THE ROUG

Cloud Computing

1st Edition

ROUGH GUIDES

www.roughguides.com

Credits

The Rough Guide to Cloud Computing

Text, design and layout: Peter Buckley
Editors: Kate Berens, Matthew Milton
Proofreading: Jason Freeman
Production: Rebecca Short

Rough Guides Reference

Director: Andrew Lockett
Editors: Kate Berens, Peter Buckley,
Tracy Hopkins, Matthew Milton,
Joe Staines, Ruth Tidball

Publishing information

This first edition published February 2010 by
Rough Guides Ltd, 80 Strand, London, WC2R 0RL
Email: mail@roughguides.com

Distributed by the Penguin Group:
Penguin Books Ltd, 80 Strand, London, WC2R 0RL
Penguin Group (USA), 375 Hudson Street, NY 10014, USA
Penguin Group (Australia), 250 Camberwell Road, Camberwell, Victoria 3124, Australia
Penguin Group (Canada), 90 Eglinton Avenue East, Suite 700, Toronto, Ontario, Canada M4P 2Y3
Penguin Group (New Zealand), Cnr Rosedale and Airborne Roads, Albany, Auckland, New Zealand

Printed and bound in Singapore

Typeset in Minion and Gill Sans

The publishers and author have done their best to ensure the accuracy and currency of all information in
The Rough Guide to Cloud Computing; however, they can accept no responsibility for any loss or inconvenience
sustained by any reader as a result of its information or advice.

224 pages; includes index

A catalogue record for this book is available from the British Library.

ISBN 13: 978-1-84836-520-9

1 3 5 7 9 8 6 4 2

THE ROUGH GUIDE to

Cloud Computing

Peter Buckley

ROUGH
GUIDES

www.roughguides.com

Contents

Part 3: Work in the cloud

Part 4: Play in the cloud

The 100 websites that will change your life...

About this book

Why a book about cloud computing?

Like the meteorological phenomena from which it takes its name, "cloud" computing is not a static, pocketable thing that can be defined quickly before moving on (though I shall have a stab at doing just that over the following pages). Instead, it is, well, cloud-like in its scope and hue. There are many shades of grey and many ways of pinning down the concept; but all incarnations share one common thread – the internet. That's what cloud computing is all about: using the internet in new and exciting ways to unshackle our daily computing experience from a single machine, in a single room, using only the tools that we happen to have installed on our PC or Mac.

As the author of *The Rough Guide to The Internet*, I have been in a prime position to watch the internet and the world wide web evolve over time and, arguably, the most important contributors to that evolution have been the increasing power of personal computing hardware and the explosion of fast, reliable, always-on internet connections. The end result is that we can now buy, sell, communicate, work and play on the internet in a way that we simply couldn't a decade ago.

Perhaps the most familiar example of web-based cloud computing in action is email. Once upon a time, we composed our emails "off-line" using a mail application. When we were all set with a bag of messages ready to send, we'd connect our lightning-fast dial-up modem and hit the "Send & Receive" button (being sure not to stay connected for too long, given that back then internet access, like regular phone calls, was charged by the minute). In contrast, today's email comes and finds us, pushing its way through permanently connected broadband connections and even reaching devices in our pockets across mobile phone networks.

Taken to the next level, you could today choose to employ cloud services to create text documents online, manage spreadsheets, create music, keep track of your finances, access your music collection, manage all your contacts and calendars, do your weekly shopping, stay in touch with friends and family … the list really does go on and on.

With so many cloud services and functions available, you probably won't embrace every site or tool in this book with equal zeal. But one thing that all the websites covered in these pages do is change our relationship to digital media – by which I mean everything from emails and document files to photo collections, digital music and blog (or micro-blog) posts – allowing us new freedoms to shape and control our experience online.

More importantly, cloud computing is allowing our real world and web lives to mesh in increasingly interesting ways, to the point that we find ourselves using services via smartphones and netbooks without really thinking of it as having anything to do with "the internet". You may already take it for granted that an email is as quick and convenient to send as an SMS text, or that the latest football results are just a click away. However you use the internet now, though, you can look to take it another step and try something new. There is nothing particularly "techie" about using an online to-do list, or placing your groceries order via the web on your mobile phone – it can be very liberating, leaving you with more time to do the things you want to do. Like writing a book, perhaps?

Note!

The internet is a continuously evolving entity, and websites come and go via the web equivalent of natural selection. Equally, it is not uncommon for larger websites and online services to swallow up the smaller ones that show a spark of originality and then take the functionality for their own. Nowhere is this likely to be more true than in the world of cloud computing, where new start-ups and household names are already jostling for position. The bottom line is that some of the sites covered in this book may well fall by the wayside, change their names or be absorbed by the Googles and Apples of this world.

If you find that a particular link no longer works, try googling to see where the service might have moved to, or dig around for the company's biography on Wikipedia (*wikipedia.org*) – always a good place to find out who's bought who.

With regard to software and functionality, also keep in mind that websites, browsers and apps often change their layout, so references to specific commands may in some instances have changed or moved to a different part of a site.

Part 1: Cloud basics

01

FAQs: frequently asked questions

Everything you wanted to know but were afraid to ask

The bulk of this book is devoted to previewing the coolest and most useful web-based applications and services currently available. However, before we get into the nitty-gritty of what's out there, let's address all those general questions that you've already asked yourself (and some that you probably haven't) about the world of cloud computing. You'll find more details on many of these subjects later on.

Basics

What exactly is cloud computing?

The term "cloud computing" has been around for a while and can be taken to mean slightly different things. In the world of IT, the phrase encompasses several shades of meaning, all revolving around the idea of providing specific, on-demand services (applications, email, etc) to multiple customers across a network. In short, taking the onus away from the individual's personal computer or work station, and placing the resources that provide that service remotely … in the cloud. In many firms, therefore, the "cloud" is shorthand for the company's central network servers and the services they provide. Another example of a closed, private cloud setup would be a public library system, where all the terminals feed from a central database that lets you browse what's available and book items in and out … are you still awake?

Sorry … I think I'm at the wrong party!

Hold your horses. Though there are loads of books out there that deal with the techie, IT side of cloud computing, this isn't one of them. These pages are devoted to the type of cloud computing that we can all plug into over the internet – itself a gigantic global network of computers. Taking our definition of cloud computing to the next level, what we're concerned with are the web-based applications and services that place the tools and data we need on the internet, making them available to us anywhere that we can get online … whether that be at home, at work, out and about with a laptop or netbook, or even sitting on the beach with an internet-capable smartphone.

This is in contrast to traditional "desktop" computing, where the applications we use and documents we create are largely stored on a single machine in our homes.

Is cloud computing just another name for Web 2.0 services?

Yes and no. The two concepts are closely linked, but they have developed slightly different meanings within the internet community. The "Web 2.0" label was originally coined back in 2004 by Tim O'Reilly, a champion of open source software development. And though you might be forgiven for thinking that it referred to a brand shiny new internet to replace the old one (as you might expect if 2.0 was tagged on the end of a piece of software's moniker), instead it describes the arrival of innovative new websites – social networking sites such as MySpace and Facebook being the most obvious examples – that have changed the very nature of the world wide web, and in turn our relationship to it. Cloud computing, meanwhile, is from our perspective a tag for the services and experiences to be had from this innovative, exciting and ever-evolving world wide web.

Has this all got something to do with Google?

There are countless companies out there developing innovative cloud computing tools, but as for how many of them will still be around a few years from now, you don't need a crystal ball to deduce that many will probably fall by the wayside while a handful of larger players swallow them up and jostle for our attention. No doubt Google, Microsoft and Apple will be among those key players as the world of cloud computing develops, a proposition that has raised serious questions about how desirable it is for such large organizations to hold so much of our personal data.

Google, for one, are being watched very carefully by both their advocates and those more critical of the company's reach and power. There is no ignoring the fact that they have expanded their portfolio in recent years to include a lot more than simply web searches. Nearly everyone reading this book will have heard of Google Mail, aka Gmail (among the most popular web- or cloud-based email services, and by far the best; see p.82). Alongside Gmail, the company's ever-expanding suite of tools includes Google Bookmarks (see p.114), Google Docs (see p.138), YouTube (see p.176), Google Voice (see p.86), the iGoogle homepage (see p.129), Google Calendar (see p.92), Google Maps (see p.196) and Google Earth (see p.197).

The Google Opt Out Village

For an entertaining swipe at the big company with the colourful logo, tune in to *The Onion*'s spoof news story about a remote "Opt Out Village", open to anyone who doesn't feel quite ready to dive head first into the Google cloud. Point your browser at: *theonion.com/content/video/google_opt_out_feature_lets_users*.

Hang on. Google Earth isn't a web-based application is it?

Well spotted. Google Earth is a traditional application in that it needs to be downloaded and installed on your computer before it can be used. However, like several of the other services mentioned in this book (Evernote and Skype, to name but two), Google Earth's computer-and phone-based applications do not negate the fact that the internet provides the meat-and-gravy of the experience, and that these services enable you to personalize them in such a way that you can pick up where you left off, from any number of machines, any time, over any internet connection.

Many of the names mentioned in this book (such as eBay and YouTube) might at first glance appear to be traditional old-school websites, however, the tools and personalizable experience that they provide warrants them a perch on the cloud computing family tree. So, "cloud computing" is really all about how we incorporate the internet into our lives. Where once the world wide web provided a largely passive experience (you hopped from page to page reading the information you needed), today it is far more interactive and from the individual's point of view, eminently customizable.

So, what can cloud computing do?

With the rate at which these new web-based technologies are developing, the question might better be phrased as what *can't* cloud computing do. If you can think of something that you would like to be able to do online, then chances are that someone else has already had that same thought and put the tools in place. And though that might include everything from online simultaneous equation calculators (numberz.co.uk) to tools for choosing colour schemes (kuler.adobe.com), cloud computing is at its most powerful when dealing with the stuff we take for granted: sending messages, organizing our calendars, making shopping lists, getting some work done, listening to music, watching movies. Here are a few more pointers to give you an idea of how web-based cloud computing can change your life. With the services covered in these pages, you can:

- ► **Keep your contacts and calendars in sync** See p.91

- ► **Read news and email on the train** See p.90

- ► **Edit and crop your photos** See p.149

- ► **Listen to your favourite tunes** See p.167

- ► **Collaboratively write and edit documents** See p.137

- ► **Create a virtual desktop** See p.127

- ► **Remember what you should be doing** See p.99

- ►**Automatically back up important files** See p.70

- ► **Host a web conference** See p.146

- ► **Find your way around** See p.195

- ► **Share your bookmarks with the world** See p.107

- ► **Record music online** See p.174

- ► **Design your own font** See p.148

- ► **Make free phone calls** See p.87

- ► **Become a "Jam Legend"** See p.201

Why would I want to use the internet for any of this?

We have already hinted at many of the benefits of working, and playing, online in the cloud. First of all, it means that you can strip away some of the software you have installed on your PC or Mac at home in favour of web-based alternatives. This, in theory, should improve your computer's general performance. More importantly, however, by computing in the cloud you are unshackling yourself from that desktop machine, so that you can access all your email, files, music, pictures and more, from wherever you are, using whatever web-friendly device you have to hand, keeping you well and truly in the loop, 24/7.

Do I still need a computer?

Yes – or at the very least you need access to one. The majority of the tools and services mentioned in this book are available via regular computer browser software (see p.16) – Internet Explorer, Safari and Firefox being the most popular choices – which can be run on anything from a full-blown desktop machine to a laptop or inexpensive netbook (such as the pictured model, manufactured by Asus). Though rarely as powerful as desktop or laptop machines, netbooks are becoming increasingly popular not only thanks to their relative cheapness, but also because they are eminently portable and well-suited for use with web-based tools. For more on netbooks, see p.45. The alternative is to invest in a so-called smartphone with internet access, for more on which, turn to p.48.

Is my current computer up to the job?

If you bought a PC or Mac in the last few years, it will more than likely be capable of getting you online to use cloud computing tools. In fact, assuming that you use the internet in some way or other, you are already in the game. However, once you start using internet services to stream music and video or employ some of the more powerful, graphics-based tools available, you might find that either your hardware or internet connection (see p.30) is letting you down. For more on choosing the right machine, turn to p.12; for more on internet connections, see p.30.

Does it matter whether I use a Mac or a PC?

On the whole, no. Given that cloud services are generally deployed via a web browser, the platform on which that browser is running is academic – it might be Microsoft's Windows on a PC, OS X on a Mac, or perhaps some flavour of the Linux operating system. That said, you might still occasionally come across specific websites or services that are not compatible with Apple Macs running OS X. These are more often than not sites that stream TV content and have not yet expanded the video formats they supply to accommodate Macs.

Whatever operating system you use, the more important thing is that all your software is up to date. To find out how to do this for both Apple Macs and Windows PCs, turn to p.57.

Which browser should I use?

If you own a Windows PC, you may well be used to working with Internet Explorer, and if you have a Mac, the resident browser is named Safari. But these are not the only players on the field, and the increasingly popular Mozilla Firefox is an excellent alternative with loads of scope for customization, while Google's Chrome also has some nice features and a very clean look. For an in-depth discussion of the current browsers worth considering, turn to p.16.

What's all this I've read about a Google operating system?

At the time of writing, Google are gearing up to release their very own computer operating system, called Chrome, like their web browser. Chrome is the first computer operating system that has been built with cloud computing in mind. In short, it has none of the waste associated with traditional desktop computing, making it incredibly quick to boot up and perfect for use on netbooks.

What's more, because Google are distributing Chrome to developers as an open source concern (which, among other things, means that it's free to use), netbooks that will eventually be sold with Chrome pre-installed are likely to be significantly cheaper

Google Chrome Blog

Computer requirements

Any Mac or PC produced in the last couple of years, including laptops, should be fine for getting you online and using web-based tools and services, and many older machines will also work. But it's certainly worth checking your hardware before you get started. The core requirements for a great internet experience are a recent operating system, a fast internet connection at home, and, if you intend to take the machine out and about, the necessary hardware to get connected on the move.

► **Operating system** To check what operating system you have on a PC, right-click the **My Computer** icon and select **Properties**. If you have Windows Me, 98 or 95, you could consider upgrading to XP, Vista or Windows 7, but it will cost you (from $99/£70), it can be a bit of a headache and you'll need to check whether your hardware is up to the job (see *microsoft.com/windows*). Realistically, it's probably worth considering a new machine as you might have trouble running the most recent versions of the more popular web browsers. Whatever you have, make sure you download the latest updates from Microsoft via **Windows Update** in the **Start Menu**. On a Mac, select **About This Mac** or **System Profiler** from the **Apple Menu**. Upgrading to the latest version of OS X (v10.6, Snow Leopard) costs as little as $29/£19. But first check the minimum requirements to make sure your machine can handle the new operating system (see *apple.com/macosx*). It's worth noting that Snow Leopard only works on Intel Macs, and does not support any older PowerPC-based Macs.

►**Wireless connectivity** Nearly all laptop and desktop machines these days feature Wi-Fi capabilities, allowing you to connect to a wireless router in the home or wireless hotspots when out and about. If your machine doesn't, then the functionality can be added with an inexpensive adapter. It is also possible to set up a laptop to connect directly to cellphone providers' data networks, though the charges can be quite steep. For more on all these options, turn to p.48.

► **Hard drive space** Given that cloud computing is all about taking your digital life off your own computer, you could take the decision to go the whole way and store all your photos and documents online (see p.181 and p.117), manage email online (see p.81), and even stream music from the web (see p.167), negating the need for you to store anything much locally. A few years from now such a setup might well be the norm, but today you will more than likely still want to keep at least a copy of your photos, music and the like to hand at home. To find out how big and how full your hard drive is on a PC, open **My Computer**, right-click the C-drive icon and select **Properties**. On a Mac, right-click your hard drive icon on the desktop and select **Get Info** from the context menu that appears. If you think you are going to need more space, try deleting any large files that you no longer need (or burning them to CDs) and then empty the Recycle Bin or Trash. On a PC, you could also try running the Disk Cleanup utility: right-click the C-drive icon, select **Properties**, and then click the **Disk Cleanup** button. On a Mac, download OnyX (*titanium.free.fr*) to help clean things up.

▶**Webcams** Though not essential, a webcam really expands the experience of internet telephony services such as that offered by Skype (see p.87). Many machines come with one built-in above the screen (such as the Apple MacBook Pro pictured below) – a feature worth looking out for when splurging on a new computer.

For everything else you need to know about choosing, using and upgrading a PC, Mac or internet connection, see this book's sister volumes: *The Rough Guide to Windows 7*, *The Rough Guide to Macs & OS X* and *The Rough Guide to the Internet*. And for more specifics on buying a netbook, turn to p.45.

than Windows equivalents, where the latter's manufacturers are required to pay Microsoft for each Windows installation that they ship. If you want to find out more about the Chrome OS, point your browser at the Google Chrome Blog, and home in on the FAQs page: chrome.blogspot.com/2009/07/google-chrome-os-faq.html.

Do I need to change my internet connection?

If you already have a broadband internet connection at home, then all will be well. Even relatively slow broadband setups (less than 1 megabit per second) should give you a fat enough pipe to get reasonable results from most cloud-based services. Obviously, the faster your broadband, the better your online life will be, though you may decide that it is not worth paying extra each month for a faster connection when you are more than happy with what you already have. If you are using a slower dial-up connection, it is definitely time to upgrade to broadband; turn to p.30 for a few pointers.

Sounds good so far. But...

Do I really want to be connected all the time?

That's really a question that only you can answer. And though we have obviously survived as a species for quite some time without the ability to post photos to the web seconds after snapping them, that isn't in itself a reason not to get involved.

Perhaps a more helpful way to look at this question is to think about the volume of your involvement in all things cloud-related. Once you get yourself a smartphone and start signing up for multiple newsfeeds, Twitter accounts, "push" notifications (from your email, to-do lists, even eBay), you can suddenly find yourself with an awful lot of material to wade through on a daily basis. In short, there is a thin line between paddling in your personal data stream and drowning in it.

The answer? Be selective about what you sign up for, especially where it involves a commitment from your end. However much you enjoy contributing to a Twitter, Facebook or Flickr stream, it shouldn't be the thing that defines you or the way you spend all of your time.

So it might change people's expectations of me?

Yes, it might. Once you become the kind of person who picks up and responds to emails any time, anywhere, or maintains a constant stream of witty and entertaining posts online, people will expect it of you and might feel put out if you take longer than usual to respond to their messaging.

Again, the answer is to be selective about what you do online, and think carefully about whether each activity is improving your quality of life, or just contributing to a great big digital "time suck"!

What if the internet goes down?

Though the internet as a whole is never actually going to "go down" or even come close to a grinding halt, individual companies are reliant on their own servers, which are in turn connected to, and part of, the internet. When you hear about companies like Google suffering "outages" or losing service, the problem generally relates to such servers. These servers are part of vast "server

chapter 1

Choosing a web browser

Your web browser is the key component of your internet toolkit. It's not only the window through which you view webpages but a package for downloading files, viewing news feeds and much more. Your computer will almost certainly already have a web browser installed, but that doesn't mean it's necessarily the best one to use. So here's a quick run-through of the main browsers out there. Don't be afraid of trying a few out to see what suits you best – you can always uninstall them, or use different browsers for different tasks.

► **Internet Explorer** (*microsoft.com/ie*) Microsoft's Internet Explorer, or IE, is far and away the world's most widely used browser. Recent versions are decent enough, but IE's popularity is mainly down to the fact that for years it has come pre-installed on nearly every new PC as a part of Microsoft Windows. IE has traditionally trailed behind its competitors in terms of features and security. The most recent version, IE8, closed the gap somewhat, but Firefox is still a superior option.

► **Safari** (*apple.com/safari*) Pre-2005 Macs also came with IE, but the standard Mac OS X browser now is Apple's own Safari. In most ways, it's an excellent browser – especially Safari 4, the version that was released in 2009. Safari is also now available to Windows PC users. It's fast, intuitive and nice-looking, with a Google search box built in. It also features excellent tabbed browsing, top-class newsfeed tools and an iTunes-style Cover Flow view for browsing your bookmarks. Still, whether you use a Mac or PC it's worth checking out both Safari and Firefox (see below) to see which suits you better.

► **Firefox** (*getfirefox.com*) First released in 2004, Firefox is an excellent browser created by the Mozilla Foundation as an open-source product with the help of volunteer programmers around the world. Firefox has a huge range of features, and even if you discover something that it can't do, you'll often find that the desired function can be easily added via an extension or some other customization. Furthermore, most experts agree that Firefox leaves PC users slightly less vulnerable to potentially harmful scripts and other web-based nasties than does Internet Explorer. With customizable address-bar searching, excellent privacy tools and many other handy extras, this is the best choice for PC and Mac users at the time of writing.

► **Chrome** (*google.com/chrome*) Chrome is one of Google's most recent additions to its armoury, and though still very much in its infancy is definitely worth considering. One interesting feature is the fact that when you open a new tab or window in Chrome you are shown nine thumbnails of your most frequently visited sites in place of the "home" feature that most browsers use. Given Google's commitment to cloud computing tools, Chrome is sure to be an important browser to watch over the coming months and years – its integration with the rest of Google's toolbox will inevitably get slicker and more fully featured.

► **Opera** (*opera.com*) Hailing from Scandinavia, Opera introduced many now-standard features (such as tabbed and multi-page bookmarks) years before its competitors. And it still has many unique extras, such as a fully featured mail program built right into the browser window. It's also very fast and worth trying.

Important: update your browser

Whichever browser you use, be sure to keep it up to date – partly to gain any extra features, but more importantly to ensure that you're not exposing yourself to any security risks. Many people assume that as long as they don't open any dodgy email attachments, they'll be safe from viruses, hackers and other such evils, but with an out-of-date browser it's possible to catch something nasty just by visiting a malicious web-page. With recent PCs and Macs, updates will be offered automatically and should be accepted.

Browser plug-ins & add-ons

Once you start using browsers to access web-based services you will find yourself being hassled on a daily basis to download updates to browser add-ons that you might have chosen to install, as well as additional plug-ins that the browser requires to make a particular website function correctly. These are easily confused with the kind of malicious software that you really don't want to be downloading, so to help you along, here are a few things that should be safe to download:

▶ **Adobe Air** This browser plug-in is required by many recent web-based apps with a graphics-heavy interface and is well worth installing.

▶ **Adobe Flash** Another common plug-in required by many websites that feature animations, movie clips or browser-based games.

▶ **Firefox add-ons** These sometimes appear as a pop-up window when you launch the browser and generally request that you "Install and relaunch".

▶ **QuickTime** This is Apple's video player plug-in, and, again, should be downloaded without hesitation when offered.

▶ **RealPlayer** Another video player plug-in required by some websites, though not as common these days as Flash and QuickTime.

▶ **Silverlight** This is Microsoft's web application framework and, like Air, is required by many sites that employ interactive graphic elements.

farms" that hold all our cloud data and dish it up to us as and when we need it. Though we talk of "the cloud" as if it were some illusive spectral entity, it would not exist without this physical hardware that, just like your desktop computer, relies on electricity and can sometimes go wrong.

In recent times there have been several newsworthy instances when the big guns have left many thousands of individuals without email, or access to their files, for hours at a time. This can be frustrating – and costly, too, if you rely on such services for your business. Aside from the inconvenience of such outages, there have also been instances where cloud services have "lost" individuals' data. Thankfully, such occurrences are few and far between, and to be honest, any company that has ventured into the realm of cloud computing is likely doing a far more efficient job of backing up your data than you are doing yourself. At the end of the day, your personal data and files are probably more likely to be deleted, robbed or otherwise damaged within the four walls of your own home (see below) than they are while residing online.

What if my computer dies?

Hard drives occasionally give up the ghost, in which case the only chance of getting any of the contents back is a time-consuming and potentially expensive data-recovery process. And, of course, computers can meet many other nasty ends: theft, lightning, fire, spilled coffee and so on. That's what is so great, in principle, about cloud computing – all your files, emails and the like reside on the web, so as and when the unthinkable happens to your computer, it's simply a matter of getting yourself set up with another machine and then pointing it at your online data pool. Equally, when you trade in an old model for something newer, migrating becomes a whole lot less painful when all your files and tools are online anyway.

Do I need to keep both my online and offline data backed-up?

It can't do any harm. The reality of most people's systems is very different to the utopian scenario described above where

How is all my data stored?

Clever though computers are, they only deal in numbers – digital, rather than analogue, information. In fact, their vocabulary is limited to just zeros and ones: the "binary" system. So a single MP3 file or Word document is reduced to a series of millions of zeros or ones. To give you an idea, an 80GB hard drive in a computer can hold around 600 billion zeros and ones – roughly 100 for every person on the planet.

Storage capacity, either on your computer or online, is generally measured in gigabytes – also known as gigs or GBs. Roughly speaking, a byte is eight zeros and ones (the space required on a computer disk to store a single character of text) and a gigabyte is a billion bytes. A gig is the same as 1000MB (megabytes) or 1,000,000KB (kilobytes).

Mathematically minded readers may be interested to know that all these figures are actually approximations of the number two raised to different powers. A gigabyte is two bytes to the power of thirty, which equals 1,073,741,824 bytes.

But where do all these zeros and ones go once they've left your computer? Well, as has been hinted at earlier in this chapter, they zip off across the internet and find their way to the servers that happen to be hosting the service or web application that you are using. As to where that is, it could be anywhere on the planet, and unless you do some serious detective work, you are unlikely to ever know.

Many of the larger companies with cloud computing concerns (such as Google and Apple) run their own vast "data centres", also known as "server farms", while smaller start-ups might lease server space from a company that specializes in providing server real estate. In both instances, these centres house hundreds of computers and thousands of GBs of data. Resources will be spread across several distinct geographical locations, so that any problems that might arise at one site shouldn't affect the service, and even if it "goes down" from your perspective, all your data will still be safe and secure on the server.

Such centres tend to be high-security installations with access restricted to only a select few company employees. For an interesting insight into how they operate, check out *The Independent*'s article (*tinyurl.com/lulqhk*), written by Rough Guides author Rhodri Marsden.

everything lives online in complete safety – many of us keep some material online (emails, some photos perhaps) and some locally (music collections and maybe some Word documents), and given that we live in an imperfect universe, it is impossible to say that everything is going to be 100 percent secure online.

So you need to think carefully about what's where, what you might need to access if your internet connection ever failed, and how you want to use and share the material you keep online. At the end of the day it's your responsibility to make sure everything is backed up in a way that gives you piece of mind; to find out how to achieve that, turn to p.70.

Isn't it a hassle to switch from the services and tools I already use?

In many instances it is simply a matter of visiting a website, setting up an account and then getting on with it. Specific services may well have their own specific hassles, however, especially those that require you to migrate large amounts of data to the web. To get started with an image hosting service (see p.181), for example, you will more than likely want to copy all your existing photos from your computer to your new online account. Though some sites will help you automate the process, others might require you to do it image by image ... not the most fun you could be having of a weekend.

Surprisingly, switching email services is pretty straightforward these days, and is covered on p.82. The only other slight annoyance might come if you have shelled out for some desktop software that you no longer want to use. If you still have the original installation CD and box, you could always sell it on eBay and get a few pennies back.

All my friends are still using regular applications ... like Microsoft Word

Microsoft unarguably have a pretty firm grip on the world of word processing, thanks to their ubiquitous Microsoft Office suite (itself currently being reinvented for the cloud) and more specifically Microsoft Word. As a result, most cloud-based office suites (see p.137) include some kind of functionality that lets you import and/or export Word documents. With both Google Docs (see p.138) and Zoho Writer (see p.140), for example, you can export your documents in the Microsoft Word format, though if you want to share it with someone, it would probably be easier to email them an invitation to view the document for themselves online (and in turn  spread the word about the services). In short, don't fret ... there are almost always ways to bridge the gap between one system and another.

Is this all going to cost me an arm and a leg?

No. Many of the cloud services and tools in this book are free to use, with the companies that run them making money from selling ad space on their pages. Some others do charge a small fee (either a one-off payment or annual subscription), but it isn't generally very much, and you can often get away with using a free, feature-lite version until you are sure you want to sign up for a "pro" offering. You might well find that you can actually save money by sidestepping paid-for computer software in favour of web-based tools.

Aren't there security risks associated with cloud computing?

Wherever and however you store your precious data, there are going to be issues of security. Even if you choose to store all your emails, addresses, financial records and the like on your home computer, there is a danger that it might be stolen or hacked into from the web. By the same token, migrating your data to the cloud has its risks. Individual companies' servers may not be 100 percent impervious to attacks, although the greater danger comes from unscrupulous individuals finding ways to get their paws on your usernames and passwords and then using them to their own end.

The good news is that with a bit of common sense you should be able to stay safe online. Once you know what you need to be looking out for, it is relatively easy to avoid the scammers and online fraudsters. For the full story, turn to p.55.

What about when my data is moving back and forth?

Whenever you use a web-based application within a web browser you're sending data back and forth between your computer and the server hosting the service or tool. As it moves, it can in some instances be intercepted, especially if you are working via a public Wi-Fi hotspot. Someone also sharing the network can relatively easily snoop network traffic coming from your machine. This is sometimes known as sidejacking.

The answer is to use web-based services that offer protection in the form of data encryption. Gmail and Google Docs, for example, employ special protocols, which open a secured encrypted channel for the data between the Google servers and your browser. You will know when a connection is secure as the address in your browser will begin with "https://" rather than "http://". If you are in any way unsure about the security of a particular site or service, drop them a line and ask about their security features. If they can't provide you with a good answer to your enquiry, try someone else.

For more on staying safe online, turn to p.55.

Isn't this just another consumerist fad from money-grabbing corporations?

The past few years have seen some extraordinary developments in the relationship between big business and the internet. The experience of the music industry and the switch it has witnessed from physical music sales to downloads (both legal and illegal) has happened far quicker than anyone could have predicted and sent ripples of panic through many other industries.

What has become clear is that the internet, and more specifically cloud services, can offer businesses a way to make money without having to deal with traditional problems of physical manufacture and distribution. However, we are not simply looking at a shift from tangible goods to digital ones, but a fundamentally different pricing model, which for many companies is pretty horrifying.

Basically, the business model that companies such as Google have nurtured is one where tools and services are largely offered for free, but because of the incredible volume of people that have signed up, these companies are able to generate enormous amounts of revenue from relatively low-level advertising on their pages. The majority of companies cannot hope to benefit from such volumes of scale, though, and many of the start-ups currently scrabbling around for the crumbs are likely to either vanish completely, or be absorbed by larger firms over the coming years. For others, the modest subscription charge looks set to become a workable model, the hope being that once you are signed up and using the service, you'll become too reliant on it to leave.

So, in answer to the original question: no, cloud computing isn't simply a "consumerist fad" dreamed up by corporations. Rather, it is an inevitable phase in the evolution of the internet, one that has come about through the development of new

technologies that make always-on and mobile broadband a workable reality. At the time of writing it remains to be seen which companies will come out on top and which will fall by the wayside, but from a consumer's point of view, these are exciting times, with some innovative, even life-changing technologies becoming available online, many of which are free or relatively cheap to use.

02

The cloud: from home

Getting connected and staying connected

Now that exactly what cloud computing is has become a little clearer, let's take a look at a few things you should take into consideration when connecting to cloud computer services (and the internet in general) from home over a domestic internet connection. More specifically, this chapter will cover the joys of home networking, which is especially useful if your household is supporting multiple computers, phones and games consoles, all vying for a piece of the action. Getting your internet connection and networking situation sorted is an essential first step to enjoying a speedy and glitch-free cloud computing experience.

Routers & hubs

These days, many households will be supporting multiple computers, phones and other devices capable of connecting to the internet, either wirelessly or via some kind of wired connection. With this in mind, the majority of internet service providers take it for granted that when you sign up for their service, what you really need on top of the actual delivery of the broadband is a device for distributing the signal around your home – and that's where routers and hubs come into play.

Though they come in many shapes and sizes, these devices all perform the function of distributing an internet connection between two or more computers and allowing other network traffic to pass between them as well. The router connects to the internet via a modem (which may be a separate device or combined in the same unit) and each computer connects to the router, either via cables or, in the case of a wireless router, via a radio-wave technology known as Wi-Fi.

Switching ISPs

For advice on choosing an ISP, turn to p.30. If you plan to switch ISPs, remember that you may need to give a month's notice to your current provider – which can be two months in practice, if you pay at the start of the month. As with any utility supplier, switching ISPs can be something of a headache, though in the UK changing ADSL providers has become less painful thanks to a process in which each switching customer gets a Migration Authorization Code (MAC). This number has nothing to do with Apple Macs, nor MAC addresses (the "Media Access Control" numbers that allow computers to find each other on a network). It's just a code that helps ISPs provide an uninterrupted service when you switch from one account to another.

Wi-Fi networking

Wireless routers are now extremely common and many ISPs will include one when you sign up for a new account. In the UK, the typical arrangement is that the ISP sends you a wireless router along with all your login and password details. You then simply plug the router into a power source, follow a simple set of configuration instructions and then from your computer choose the relevant Wi-Fi network when it is detected. To do this on a Mac use the fan icon (at the top-right, by the clock). On a PC, if the list of available wireless networks doesn't pop up automatically, choose **Connect To** in the **Start Menu** and select the wireless option. Finally, if required, enter the password printed on a label on the bottom of the router.

Buying and setting up your own wireless router

If your ISP didn't provide a wireless router, or you want to add one to your existing broadband setup, then you'll need to purchase and set it up yourself.

Wireless routers typically cost around $75/£50. When choosing one, you first need to decide whether you need a router with a modem built in: if you already have a broadband modem that has an Ethernet socket on it, then a standard router should be fine. If not – if you have an ADSL modem with only a USB connection, for instance – then your best bet is to replace it with a router with a built-in ADSL modem.

Choosing a home internet connection

Whatever type of domestic internet access you choose, you'll need an account with an ISP (Internet Service Provider). When you connect to the net, you really connect your computer to their computer, which in turn is connected to another computer, which in turn… That's how the internet works.

The industry has matured steadily over the last decade to the point where most established ISPs deliver reasonable performance and service. However, all providers aren't equal, and it's difficult to tell good from bad until you've used them over time. Poor access will jade your online experience, so if you're not happy with the service you're getting, consider trying another.

Shopping around

When choosing an ISP, you want a reliable, fast connection and good customer support. It's definitely worth doing your own research and the best approach is to ask around – chatting with your neighbours about who they use is a great way to start. If someone swears by an ISP, and they know what they're talking about, give it a go. Of course, there's also lots of information available online, at sites such as:

Broadband.co.uk broadband.co.uk (UK)
The List thelist.com (US)
Whirlpool whirlpool.net.au (Aus)

What to ask (or at least think about)

Before signing up with any ISP, ask – or at least ponder – the following questions. Some will not apply to you, but it's worth scanning the lot just to make sure.

▶ **Is there a download limit?** If so, how much is it? And how much extra will you be charged if you download more?

▶ **Are there any other restrictions?** A few bargain ADSL providers ban file-sharing networks, for instance.

▶ **Do they throw in a free modem and/or router?** If not, how much will they charge? Can you use your own hardware?

▶ **Is there a minimum subscription period?** Some ISPs, especially budget broadband providers, require you to sign up for a minimum period – usually a year. This is standard if you receive a free modem or router when you sign up.

▶ **Can you change plan?** How much will it cost if you want to upgrade your speed or increase your download limit?

▶ **Is there a start-up, installation or activation fee?** If so, how much? And, perhaps more importantly, will they charge a cancellation fee or apply any other penalties if you ever decide to leave?

▶ **Does the package include any internet phone calls?** How much will it cost and are there any free minutes included?

▶ **What are the hours for phone support and how much does it cost?** Free phone support until the mid-evening is standard except in the UK, where rates range from national to premium.

Some major ISPs

The list below contains some of the major ISPs in Britain, North America and Australia. It's by no means complete and **inclusion shouldn't be taken as endorsement**.

UK

BT bt.com/broadband
O2 broadband.o2.co.uk
Orange orange.co.uk
Pipex pipex.net
TalkTalk talktalk.co.uk
Virgin Media virginmedia.com

North America

AT&T att.net
EarthLink earthlink.com
Golden golden.net (Can)
Inter.net inter.net (US/Can)
Verizon verizon.com

Australia

Big Pond bigpond.com
Dodo dodo.com.au

Apple's AirPort family

Historically, Apple branded their wireless-capable kit as "AirPort". The underlying technology, however, is Wi-Fi – just as with PCs – and these days even Apple have deferred to using the generic term "wireless". Whatever you want to call it, the end result is that Macs and PCs can connect to the same networks, and to each other. So feel free to mix things up on the same network.

Wi-Fi, also known by the less user-friendly name 802.11, is actually a family of slightly different standards, all of which work with each other. Most recent computers can handle 802.11n. This allows faster data transfer than the earlier 802.11g (aka AirPort Extreme) and 802.11b (aka "non-Extreme" AirPort).

Apple produces three routers – AirPort Extreme (pictured below), AirPort Express and the Time Capsule. All are wireless, nicely designed, fully featured and very easy to set up. You will, however, find that Apple's wireless hardware is more expensive than similar non-Apple devices and none of the current line-up feature their own modem – you will have to purchase one separately to use ADSL or cable broadband.

That said, there are good reasons to opt for Apple hardware, especially if you already use a Mac computer. Here are a couple more features to consider when looking at Apple wireless kit:

▶ **AirTunes** Available on the AirPort Express, AirTunes allows you to connect to a hi-fi and stream music from your PC or Mac. By default it works only with iTunes, but coupled with a third-party app called Airfoil (*rogueamoeba.com/airfoil*), it can stream audio from any application, including the cloud services covered in this book (see p.167).

▶ **Time Machine** If you have a Mac and intend to use OS X's Time Machine to manage your backups (see p.70), it's worth considering the Time Capsule, though a similar result can be achieved with a router that can connect to a network-friendly external hard drive (also known as a NAS drive).

Other things to consider are the number of Ethernet sockets and the range and speed of the wireless functions. All wireless routers will be fast enough to get the most out of your internet connection, but the latest, faster versions (such as 802.11n) can speed up file-sharing between computers (but only if the computers also have 802.11n; see box opposite).

The most established router manufacturers are Netgear, Linksys, Belkin and D-Link.

Wi-Fi security

Because Wi-Fi can work through walls, your network won't stop at your front door. This is great news for surfing in the garden, say, or sharing an internet connection among various apartments in a building. However, if the router has no security features enabled, anyone within a few hundred feet could connect to your network. They could then potentially download large files, slowing down your connection and using up your allocated monthly bandwidth; download illegal material or carry out other illegal acts that would be traceable to your ISP account; spy on your internet activity; and possibly even access personal data on your computers (see p.55).

There are two main ways to secure a wireless network. You can use one or both of these techniques.

Add a password

Some routers come with a password already set up, but in other cases you'll have to log in to the setup section of your router and configure it yourself. This usually involves opening a web browser window, entering the admin IP listed in the router's operating instructions, and looking for the relevant settings. You may find a few different types of password protection on offer:

Troubleshooting Wi-Fi

Setting up a router can be painless but it can also throw up problems. You might find that your Wi-Fi network's performance is not what it should be, or simply isn't working. Here are a few potential solutions:

▶ **Modem** If you have a separate modem, make sure it's working by connecting it directly to a computer, missing out the router.

▶ **Position** Try and position your router at the centre of your home, bearing in mind that the Wi-Fi signal transmits equally in all directions from the majority of devices – imagine a sphere of transmission with your router at the centre. Take into account the effect of large metal objects on the Wi-Fi signal; refrigerators are more often than not the guilty parties here. Also think about how close your router is to other devices that pump out radio waves, such as cordless domestic telephone base stations.

It's also worth checking the router's settings. This is usually done by "connecting" your computer (either with an Ethernet cable or wirelessly), opening a web browser window and entering the admin IP address listed in the router's instruction manual – just as if it were a website.

▶ **Wi-Fi channel** When you set up a new wireless network, your router will automatically select a "channel" to transmit on. Without getting into technicalities, most common routers tend to default to the same channels, which as a result can get rather crowded, especially in apartment blocks where there may be dozens of networks transmitting within a relatively small geographical area. Download a piece of Wi-Fi scanning software such as CoconutWiFi (*coconut-flavour.com*) for Macs or NetStumbler (*netstumbler.com*) for PCs to see which the quietest channels are around you and then log in to your router and look for the option to switch channels.

▶ **Wi-Fi flavour** Newer Wi-Fi devices tend to transmit at the faster 802.11n rate, as opposed to the older 802.11g and 802.11b standards. If you mix different flavoured devices on the same network, you may well find that your network runs at the speed of the slowest device. Some routers have a special "dual transmission" mode to deal with such situations, though you may well have to dig through the settings screens to enable it.

► **WEP** (Wired Equivalent Privacy) is offered by all routers but isn't very secure. Anyone technically minded can find and run software capable of cracking the password.

► **WPA & WPA2** (Wi-Fi Protected Access) are newer standards that are both incomparably more secure than WEP, so always choose one of these options when available.

Access lists

A WPA password is enough for most people, but for maximum security you may also want to tell your router to refuse internet access to all computers other than those you have specifically approved. You give your router an access list containing a ten-digit identity code – a so-called MAC address – for each approved computer. It then bars access to all other computers. Note that if you use an access list without a WPA password, you won't be protected from people potentially spying on your internet use.

To set things up, look for an Access List or MAC Filtering option in your router's configuration settings and enter the address of each computer. See the box (opposite) to find out how to get the addresses.

Wired networking

The traditional way to connect computers and routers is with Ethernet cables. These are very secure and reliable but can be inconvenient (and expensive) when the computers on the network are located in different rooms.

Wi-Fi, by comparison, lets you connect throughout the home and garden. It's not quite as fast or secure as Ethernet, but you'll only notice the speed difference if you're moving large files between the various computers on the network, and security

shouldn't be an issue if you follow the Wi-Fi-specific advice in this chapter.

It's perfectly possible to combine Wi-Fi and wires on the same network, and sometimes this is the most sensible thing to do. Let's say, for example, you have a desktop computer in the corner of the living room only metres away from the wireless hub that your ISP provided. Let's also say that your household boasts a couple of iPhones, a laptop and perhaps a games console – that's a lot of traffic for one Wi-Fi network to deal with, and you may well find that adding an Ethernet connection from your router to your desktop machine both improves the desktop machine's networking performance, and also frees up the airwaves for all the other Wi-Fi-capable devices in your home.

Most wireless routers offer Ethernet ports as well as a Wi-Fi signal. As for computers, most recent models have Ethernet and Wi-Fi built right in. For machines that lack one or both, inexpensive adapters are available in USB, PCI or PCMCIA formats.

Powerline networks

If the computer that you want to connect to your router is in a distant corner of your home, then Ethernet cables may well not be a practical option – they are untidy when visible and expensive to have wired into the walls. A seemingly futuristic, but very practical, alternative is powerline networking, whereby you connect your router to the electrical wiring system of your home and distribute the network signal by exploiting the miles of copper wires already hidden away within the fabric of the building. A pair of powerline adapters (like those pictured opposite) cost around £70/$140, connect to your computer and router via Ethernet cables, and then plug directly into the regular power sockets on the wall.

As with Ethernet, you can expect to achieve faster data rates than you will with Wi-Fi, and you can add multiple adapters to the same electrical system to tap into the signal from as many electrical sockets as you need to.

For more on routers and networking, see:

How Stuff Works howstuffworks.com/home-network.htm
Practically Networked practicallynetworked.com

More than one user

Once you have your network situation in hand, take a moment to think about the way the computers within your home are used and, if a specific machine is accessed by several people (often the situation if you have kids under your roof), consider setting up user accounts for those who frequently use the machine.

What's this got to do with cloud computing? Well, the point is, that if everyone using the machine has their own individual account for the various services they use (email logins, eBay account details, Spotify accounts, iTunes Store credentials, etc) then things can get pretty complicated. For example, you wouldn't want your nearest and dearest bidding away on eBay using your account details, even if it was by accident. Then there's the issue of privacy. Do you really want the rest of your family to have access to your browser history? And if you do decide to cover your tracks (see p.68), then you might also inadvertently delete the browsing history of someone else. Equally, shared browser bookmarks can become very messy and difficult to navigate. It's much better to keep things segregated.

The easiest way to ring-fence the online (and offline) computing activities of the various members of your household is with User Accounts. It might seem like a hassle at first, but it's worth getting people used to using their own accounts. Here's how to get things set up.

User Accounts in Windows

All Windows PCs will have at least one User Account set up, even if you didn't know it was there. This account will have administrator powers to make changes that can affect the system as a whole. To set up additional accounts (either Administrator or Standard), open the Windows **Control Panel** from the **Start**

Menu and click **Add or Remove User Accounts**. Next click
Create a New Account and follow the prompts. For more on User
Accounts on a Windows PC, see *The Rough Guide to Windows 7*.

User Accounts in Mac OS X

When you first got your Mac out of the box and set it up, you will
have been prompted to enter a name, "short name" and password
(and also to pick a twee little image from a selection including a
butterfly, snowflake and billiard ball). Whether you realized it or
not, you were setting yourself up with an account – and, more
specifically, an account with "administrative" powers.

Every Mac has at least one administrator – a person who
has power to make system-wide changes, install updates and

Fast User Switching

This computer function allows one user to log on without the current
user first logging off. Any documents, applications or webpages that the
current user has open stay active "in the background": hidden from view
and password-protected (assuming the account has a password). When
you switch back, everything will be as you left it.

On a Mac you can enable the feature from the Apple OS X Accounts
Login Options. Once activated, the current user's name (or a generic
icon) appears in the menu bar, next to the clock. Click here to reveal a
menu that lets you switch between users – complete with a cool cubic
pirouette.

On a PC running Windows
look within the **Control Panel**
for **User Accounts** and then
click the **Change the way users
log on or off** option.

applications, and generally be fully in control of the computer. When you add other users, you can choose whether to make them administrators (if you trust them not to do anything stupid) or standard users (great for technophobes and kids).

All the settings for User Accounts can be accessed via the **System Preferences > Accounts** pane. Here, you can add and remove accounts – if you're an administrator – using the standard "+" and "–" buttons. Once this is set up, each user will have their own browser history, preferences, bookmarks, passwords, etc. They will also have their own master password for logging into their account on the Mac. For the full story, see *The Rough Guide to Macs & OS X*.

Backing up at home

Finally, a note on backing up your home computer system – do it now! Even if you have wholeheartedly embraced the cloud computing way of life, and migrated all your precious files, photos, music and more to the web, there is always going to be the argument that you shouldn't keep all your eggs in one basket. Even if you rely on web services for your daily computing needs, it is worth regularly backing up key material to your computer, and in turn backing up the files on your computer to some kind of physically removable media – either CDs, DVDs or an external hard drive.

Both Macs and Windows PCs have their own built-in backup software. OS X's Time Machine application is very easy to use and will effortlessly create hourly, daily and weekly archives of your data via either a wired or wireless connection. This archive can then be used to retrieve lost files or even set up a new Mac.

Windows 7, meanwhile, features an application called simply Backup, which creates an "image" backup of every file and folder on your PC. This can in turn be used to restore some, or all, of your files should the worst happen.

For more on backing up options, turn to p.70.

3

The cloud: going mobile

Any time, anywhere

For many people, the fact that they can access all their emails, contacts and calendars anywhere they are via a smartphone or netbook has become a way of life. And it has to be said that, once you get used to working that way, it's hard to imagine going back. In this chapter we look at the basics of getting online away from home and examine the various mobile application platforms that are putting all aspects of the cloud in our pockets.

Public internet access

Of course, cloud computing doesn't have to involve your own hardware. Any means that you can find to get online is fair game – a public library, perhaps, or more likely an internet café.

The term "cyber café" was coined in 1994 by the proprietors of Cyberia, a small establishment in London's West End that first paired computing with cappucinos. Since then, internet cafés – with hot drinks or without – have cropped up in every corner of the globe. Today, they're mostly aimed at tourists; but others have been important, and at times controversial, sources of information for people in countries where press freedom is limited.

Though not ideally suited to all the services featured in these pages, an internet café is a great place to go to upload photos or check emails when you're out and about without hardware of your own, or if you're travelling abroad and want to avoid the cell network roaming charges that your smartphone might incur.

In many countries you'll also come across net-enabled public telephones – free or coin-operated "netbooths". When using any kind of public machine, however, make sure that any passwords and logins that you use are not remembered by the browser (or the chap sat next to you) after you leave. For more on browser security, see p.55.

Finding public access

You shouldn't have any trouble finding an internet café. There's sure to be at least one close to the main street or tourist district in any town. If not, try asking at a hotel, library or computer store. Or, if you're going abroad, check a directory before you go:

Cybercafé Guide netcafes.com
EasyInternetCafé easyinternetcafe.com

Laptops & netbooks

Over the last two decades, the internet has become an increasingly mobile phenomenon, a trend that has accompanied the growth in ownership of laptop and netbook machines (which, together, now shift more units than traditional desktop computers). The coming years are likely to see the bulk of on-the-move web browsing taking place on phones with internet functionality (see p.48).

As an internet station in your home, a laptop or netbook computer works exactly like a standard desktop machine. But laptops are designed to be taken on the road, and they can be connected to the net in various ways when you're away from home:

Connecting via Wi-Fi

With a laptop or PDA (personal digital assistant) that has wireless capability you can connect anywhere you find an accessible Wi-Fi network. This might be at a friend's house, café, hotel, or even using a city-wide network.

Though none are comprehensive, there are various online directories of hotspots, such as:

WeFi wefi.com
Wi-Fi Free Spot wififreenet.com

There are also many downloadable apps for Windows, Macs and smartphones that will help you find out whether there is any

Wi-Fi nearby. WeFi offer a good range. A smartphone app can be particularly useful, as it will enable you to track down hotspots via your cell provider's data network long before your laptop gets in range of any Wi-Fi nearby.

Many commercial hotspots are pay-to-use. You either pay the person running the system (over the counter in a café, for instance) or sign up directly via your laptop. If you use such services a lot, you may save time and money by signing up with a service such as Boingo, T-Mobile or AT&T's Wayport, which allow you to connect at thousands of hotspots for a monthly fee.

Boingo boingo.com
T-Mobile t-mobile.com/hotspot
Wayport wayport.com

Many hotspots, however, provide free access for all. Some businesses do this intentionally, others simply by having an unencrypted network that a laptop user can sniff out and use from the pavement outside. (Motoring around to find free Wi-Fi points, whether from hotspots, homes or unwitting offices, is known as wardriving.)

Buying a netbook

Only a few years ago the idea of mini-laptops was a novelty; now they have really taken off, and are so affordable that many people purchase one to supplement a high-powered home machine, or larger laptop. In terms of portability they can't be beaten, but there are several considerations that have to be taken into account when making your choice.

▶ **Size** With regular laptops, their overall size is generally described in terms of the diagonal screen size – 13" or 15" for example. It's the same with netbooks. The smaller screened models (9" rather than 10", say) will generally have compromised on the keyboard size to achieve the smaller profile. With this in mind, always make sure you have a play with the model before you commit – there are few things more frustrating than an uncomfortable keyboard.

▶ **Screen quality** As above, always make sure that you get a chance to see the netbook in action before you buy, as screens can really vary in quality. Is it crisp and clear? Are the colours bright? What's the angle of view like?

▶ **Drive type** Traditionally, computer storage drives have been mechanical hard drives (HDs), which contain magnetic discs read by a small arm that moves back and forth, much like that of a record-playing turntable. These days, however, many laptop and netbook manufacturers offer solid state drives (SSDs), which use memory chips similar to those found in digital cameras and most MP3 players. Because they have no moving parts, they are far less susceptible to damage by being bashed around (compared to HDs), but they rarely offer the same capacity as regular drives and are considerably more expensive.

▶ **Brand** Don't feel compelled to go with a name brand. Though many of the larger computer manufacturers are rushing to bring netbooks to the marketplace, they also tend to charge a bit of a premium for their name. One company worth checking out is Asus (eeepc.asus.com) and their Eee PC range.

▶ **Price** Taking into account what has already been said about brands, it is still fair to say that you get what you pay for with netbooks, so look carefully at the specs when comparing prices, and if you can afford a little more, it will likely be a sound investment.

Connecting via an Ethernet cable

Most modern laptops have a built-in Ethernet port. This will usually be all you need to get online via an office network, and it can also allow you to share an internet connection at a friend's house where there's no wireless network. Simply plug a network cable between their computer and your laptop, turn on Connection Sharing (in Windows 7 go to **Control Panel > Network and Internet > Network and Sharing Center**; on a Mac, it's in **System Preferences > Sharing**), and you have an impromptu network, allowing you both to be online at the same time. If your laptop lacks an Ethernet socket, you can add one with an inexpensive adapter – either PCMCIA or USB.

Connecting through a mobile internet account

An increasingly common – and increasingly affordable – option for laptop users is a mobile internet account from one of the major cell service providers.

For roughly the same amount of money as a domestic broadband account you get your internet service supplied over the GPRS and 3G airwaves, generally via a USB device called a dongle (which, like the device pictured right, looks very much like a USB flash drive), but sometimes in the form of a PCMCIA card. Such services give you internet access pretty much anywhere that you can get a phone signal, and the download speeds are significantly faster than those achieved by smartphones and PDAs

Dongles at home

If you do sign up for a mobile internet contract from one of the major cell networks, you might also be able to use it to satisfy your domestic internet needs as well as out and about. If you have multiple machines at home, look for accounts that come with a special Wi-Fi router (pictured right) that the USB dongle can plug straight into, enabling you to share the connection over a network.

using the same networks. On the downside, most cell service providers currently offer relatively stingy download caps and long tie-in periods – an unattractive prospect for a technology anticipated to drop in price rapidly over the next couple of years.

One other advantage of a mobile internet account is that you can use the dongle both when you are out and about and when you are at home (see box above).

An even neater alternative for getting a laptop connected anywhere with a mobile internet account is a machine that comes GPRS – or 3G – ready. Such laptops have a SIM card and antenna built in and when you buy the laptop you sign up for a contract. This setup is primarily aimed at the business market at present and, as you might expect, is not cheap, especially if you travel and want to use overseas networks. In Europe, both Dell and HP have hooked up with Vodafone to offer such a service, so visit their sites to find out more.

Phones & PDAs

Internet-capable phones range widely in terms of useability and features. Plain-old mobile phones with WAP (Wireless Application Protocol) are now considered to be feeding close to the bottom of the gadget pool – hence common alternative interpretations of the acronym, such as "Worthless Application Protocol" and "Wait And Pay". Keep your expectations low, or you'll be disappointed.

More recent so-called "smartphones" and PDAs (personal digital assistants) based on EDGE, GPRS (sometimes dubbed "2.5G") and, even better, 3G (Third Generation, also called

"Tethering" via a cellphone

It is possible to connect a laptop to the internet via a cellphone – a process that's often referred to as "tethering".

The basic requirement is a data-compatible handset, ideally one with fast connection technology such as GPRS or 3G. You also need some way to connect the phone to the computer. This might be a cable, possibly in conjunction with a special modem. But a slicker option is to connect the phone and computer wirelessly using Bluetooth. Bluetooth is featured on most recent laptops and data-compatible phones, allowing them to talk to each other quickly and reliably; inexpensive USB adapters are available for older laptops.

Ask in any phone shop to get the full lowdown. Your cell network provider may well offer a special tethering tariff, though don't be surprised if you have to pay through the nose for it. Some cell service providers, however, frown upon tethering. Even if your mobile is data compatible and even if you can get it working without their consent, you might quickly run up some hefty usage bills, or even find that you have broken the terms of your cell contract.

A similar option is to get either a PCMCIA card or USB dongle 3G mobile internet account (see p.46).

UMTS) are much better, some of them offering a fully featured web browser (see box overleaf), decent connection speeds and Wi-Fi connectivity. And with potential data speeds as fast as many home broadband connections, these technologies look set to revolutionize the way we access data on the move.

After years of rip-off prices, mobile internet is finally priced quite cheaply. A phone contract that includes unlimited internet as well as many free calls costs approximately double the price of a home broadband connection.

The best and best-known web-browsing phone at the time of writing is Apple's iPhone (pictured above), which offers a 3G data connection, a super-high-res screen and a web browser that's easy to use and can do almost anything. The iPhone also has a great mail program, a

handy Google Maps tool and many other internet features. The BlackBerry, popular with corporate types, is another choice with a strong toolkit, as is the Palm Pre (pictured left), which may yet prove to be the first phone to have appeared in recent times worthy of the title "iPhone Killer".

For much more information on Apple's super-phone, see *The Rough Guide to the iPhone*. Also visit:

Apple iPhone apple.com/iphone
BlackBerry blackberry.com
Palm Pre palm.com

Mobile browsers

In many cases, mobile devices come with their own default built-in browser, so you don't need to make a choice. Some platforms, however, have several contenders worthy of note. These are among the best:

► **Mobile Safari** (*apple.com/iphone*) Used by the Apple iPhone and iPod touch, Safari displays webpages pretty much as they appear on a computer, but lacks support for Flash. There have been other browser apps made available for the iPhone, but none as yet deserve a recommendation.

► **Opera Mini** (*opera.com/mini*) This browser is intuitive and does a good job of reformatting webpages for mobile screen sizes. If you use Windows Mobile it's an excellent alternative to Microsoft's default IE Mobile browser.

► **Pre Web** (*palm.com*) Having followed the good example of Mobile Safari, the Palm Pre's built-in browser (pictured) is top-notch. It displays pages as the internet intends and is lightning fast.

► **Fennec** (*wiki.mozilla.org/ Fennec*) The Fennec browser is the cut-down version of the splendid Firefox (see p.16) and though still in "beta", will be one to watch. Versions for Symbian OS and Nokia phones are also in the pipe.

For the full story on all these and more, visit: *en.wikipedia.org/ wiki/Mobile_browser*.

App platforms

When choosing between the various smartphones on offer, it is worth looking beyond the actual hardware these days, and even beyond the software functions you get straight out of the box: these days, it's all about the "apps", or "applications".

Just as you might download software to your Mac or PC to expand its functionality, there are several unique platforms out there for downloading apps to phones to broaden their horizons. And while this book is really all about ditching traditional software in favour of web-based computing, mobile web browsers (see box opposite) tend to be limited in scope, which has in turn opened up a market for cheap, intuitive apps that offer access to specific cloud-based tools and services. As examples, Facebook, MySpace and eBay can all be navigated using a mobile web browser; each, however, produce free apps that make accessing their services quick and easy.

Many of the services and sites covered in these pages offer an app for one or more of the major platform-specific app repositories listed below:

iTunes App Store

The App Store offers everything from free utilities to fully fledged versions of computer games, which, as you might expect, will cost you a few bucks (paid through your iTunes account). The App Store can be accessed either direct from an iPhone or iPod touch, or through iTunes on a Mac or PC. To take a look at what's on offer, open iTunes and click the iTunes Store icon in the sidebar and then click through to the App Store department. Anything you download will be synced across to your iPod touch or iPhone when you connect it to your computer.

One of the best features of the App Store is that as and when developers release updates for their software, you will automatically be informed of the update and given the option to install it for free, even if you had to shell out for the original download.

Android Market

While the iTunes App Store now boasts over 65,000 apps, Android Market only has around 10,000. But this number is likely to increase rapidly, given that Android is the preferred platform for many third-party developers (especially those who have not enjoyed a particularly sunny relationship with the notoriously slow iTunes App Store approval system). Many apps on Android are free, with

Google Checkout being the only means of getting your paws on paid-for apps. Though there is a website (android.com/market), downloads are handled via handsets running Android.

BlackBerry App World

Still very much in its infancy, the BlackBerry App World doesn't yet have the range of either the iTunes or Android stores. Though things are starting to change, its content is still very much skewed toward the business user. When money does need to change hands, it is done using PayPal. To get an idea of exactly what they have in the store, visit appworld.blackberry.com/webstore.

Ovi Store

Though it might be the Apple iTunes App Store that gets all the media's attention, at the end of the day, iPhones constitute only a tiny percentage of the total number of handsets out in the world. Nokia are still one of the largest players in the mobile market and, as such, their app repository is not to be ignored. The Ovi Store has a slick interface, and all the names you'd expect to find there are represented. To find out more, visit: store.ovi.com.

Others...

There are loads of other application repositories out there at the time of writing, though several are expected to fade away, or merge as larger network operators consume their smaller competitors. To keep an eye on who's doing what, point your browser at: en.wikipedia.org/wiki/List_of_digital_distribution_platforms_for_mobile_devices.

4

Security & safety

Playing it safe online

The internet may be the greatest wonder of the modern world, but it does come with certain downsides. Increased access to information is great, but not if the information other people are accessing is yours – and private. Of course, there are threats to privacy and security in the real world, but on the internet things are rather different, not least because the wrongdoer may take the form of a piece of software entirely invisible to the victim: a virus that damages your files, say, or a keylogger that keeps a record of the usernames and passwords you type into webpages and then sends them to someone on the other side of the world. But worry not: if you follow the advice in this chapter, you – and your precious cloud data – should be fine.

The bad guys

The villains that threaten your files and privacy fall into two categories: bad software, known as malware, and bad people, known as hackers – the individuals who want to break into your computer or steal your data, passwords and online identity. Whether you're using specific cloud services or not, as an internet user, you need to be aware of the potential dangers online.

Malware

Malware is short for "malicious software", which pretty well sums up what it is: computer code written with the express purpose of doing something harmful or invasive:

▶ **Viruses** are programs that infect other program files so that they can spread from machine to machine. In order to catch a virus you must run an infected program. There are thousands of strains, most of which are no more than a nuisance, but some are capable of setting off a time bomb that could destroy the contents of your hard drive.

▶ **Worms**, like viruses, are designed to spread. But rather than wait for a computer user to transfer the infected file, they actively replicate themselves over a network such as the internet. They might send themselves to all the contacts in your email address book, for example.

▶ **Trojans** (short for Trojan horses) are programs with a hidden agenda. When you run the program it will do something unexpected, often without your knowledge. There are dozens of known Trojans circulating the internet, most with the express purpose of opening a back door to your computer to let hackers in.

▶ **Spyware**, which may arrive via a Trojan, is software designed to snoop on your computing activity. Most commonly it's planted by some kind of marketeer, who wants to find out about your online surfing and

Security: PCs vs Macs

Though less widely discussed than the fact that Apple Macs are much cooler-looking objects than PCs, a significant Mac advantage is the fact that they expose their users to far fewer security risks. This isn't because there's anything fundamentally invulnerable about Apple's OS X operating system or Mac programs in general: it's mainly because Mac users are simply in the minority. Since PCs running Windows are so ubiquitous, this is the platform that most malicious programmers focus their efforts on (and understand best). Most Mac users have never suffered a virus or any other malicious program, and the major malware outbreaks that periodically rock the PC world are unheard of among Mac users, most of whom don't even bother running virus software. If Apple succeed in making a serious indent in the PC market share, however, this will all probably change. But for now, Mac users need to be much less vigilant than PC users.

spending habits – usually to sell to someone else. But in theory it might also be installed by someone with physical access to your computer who wants to keep an eye on you or even record the keystrokes when you log in to an internet banking or shopping site.

Preventative medicine

That all adds up to a pretty intimidating list, but don't despair – there are various measures you can take to ensure that your data and privacy remain intact.

Keep your system up to date

Many security breaches involve a programmer taking advantage of a security flaw in Windows or a web browser. So it's critically important to keep your system up to speed with the latest security updates. If you don't, simply connecting to the internet or viewing a webpage could be enough to let in some kind of malware.

Recent versions of Windows and Mac OS, and web browsers such as Firefox, will automatically prompt you to download periodic updates.

Don't run dodgy software

This includes steering clear of free downloads from websites which seem in any way untrustworthy, or which you reached via a pop-up or banner ad. It also means thinking carefully before opening suspicious email attachments, even from people you know – the message may have been sent by a piece of software without them ever knowing about it.

Hide behind a firewall

A firewall serves to prevent anyone from even being able to detect your computer on the internet, let alone invade it. Recent versions of Windows come with a basic firewall built in, which will be activated by default. You can check by opening **Control Panel > Security Center**.

As for Macs, OS X comes with a pretty decent firewall installed; to check its status, or define what traffic it will or won't allow through, open **System Preferences > Sharing > Firewall** and then hit **Advanced** to fine-tune the settings (pictured). There are various other products out there, but it's certainly not imperative that you use one of them.

If you use a network router (see p.28), then you may well find that it has its own firewall. If this is enabled then you can happily turn off the firewall software of any computers on the network, as they are hidden from view by the router's firewall.

Scan regularly

Virus-scanning software keeps track of your computer activity to protect you from viruses, Trojans, worms and other such evils. No scanning software is 100 percent effective, but it does add an extra layer of security to your PC. (There are also scanners available for Macs, but for now risks seem too low to make them worth paying for.) Many PCs come with a trial from one of the major commercial scanning systems. However, you could instead opt for the free, but perfectly good, scanner offered by AVG.

AVG Free free.grisoft.com

You may also want to download and run SpyBot Search & Destroy, a free program for identifying and removing spyware:

SpyBot Search & Destroy safer-networking.org

Online virus scans

If you don't have any anti-virus software (or if the package you do have is out of date or not working) and you think you may have contracted something nasty, you could try a free online scan at the following web-sites:

TrendMicro HouseCall housecall.trendmicro.com
McAfee FreeScan freescan.mcafee.com
Symantec Security Check security.symantec.com

Enable wireless security

If you have a wireless router at home, be sure to implement
a few basic security measures. First, add a WPA password, as
described on p.33, to make sure your connection is only used
by the people you want to use it. Next, make sure you set your
own username and password for accessing your router settings
(a separate setting from the password needed to connect to the
router and use the internet). Otherwise, anyone within range
could log in, mess up your settings and even turn off your
password. All these settings are most commonly configured via
a web browser (see p.34).

Consider switching browser & mail program

Many of the "virus" crises and other problems that have caused
grief for internet users in recent years have relied on the fact
that the majority of people use Microsoft's default web browser
(Internet Explorer) and email client (Mail or Outlook Express).
You're likely to be less at risk if you switch to alternatives – the
most obvious choices being Firefox or Safari (see p.16) for your
browser and Gmail (see p.82) for email.

Secure your connections

Whenever entering sensitive data (passwords, usernames and
the like) into a webpage, make sure that the address at the top of
the browser begins "https://" rather than simply "http://". The "s"
signifies a secure connection that uses the so-called SSL (Secure
Sockets Layer) or newer TLS (Transport Layer Security) protocols.
Equally, you might also want to check whether the various
cloud services you use employ secure connections. Though it
may not matter for many sites, once you get into the realm of

Securing Gmail

Though there is still a level of inconsistency around the amount of security offered by Google between different tools in the Google suite, they do offer fully encrypted email service for the whole time that you are connected to your Gmail account through a web browser. To enable the SSL feature for your account, click **Settings** and then under the **General** tab check the **Always use https** check box; then click **Save changes** at the bottom and reload Gmail.

creating presentations online or storing sensitive documents in the cloud, you need to know that they are moving safely between your browser and the host server. If you are at all unsure about a specific service, drop them a line and ask for some clarity. If they don't give you a satisfactory response, use a different service.

Don't respond to spam

Those "get paid to surf", "stock tips", "work from home", "recruit new members", "clear your credit rating" and various network-marketing schemes are always too good to be true. If you get one of the notorious messages inviting you to take part in an African money-laundering scam, beat them at their own game:

flooble.com/fun/reply.php

Money matters

Financial aggregators

Many of us use internet banking and will regularly log in to our bank's website to check a balance, set up a direct debit or make a money transfer. Taking the service several steps further are online financial aggregator sites, which are becoming increasingly popular, particularly in the US. Their premise is that if all your investments, bank accounts, credit cards and loans can be managed by a single online portal, financial planning and budgeting become far more manageable.

Mint.com is arguably the best proposition in the US right now. The site logs into all your accounts on a daily basis and presents all your transactions for you in one place; it can even do some clever things, such as automatically tagging certain kinds of transaction as tax deductible and alerting you if any large, irregular transactions are made (a useful means of identifying fraud). Wesabe is another strong option and handles your login details differently to Mint.com: without going into the techie details, the bottom line is that your logins are stored locally on your computer rather than on the Wesabe server, which could well be a deal-clincher for many people.

Mint mint.com (US)
Wesabe wesabe.com (US)

Aggregators have not taken off in the UK in the same way that they have in the US, largely because of financial regulations that limit the ability of a website to harvest banking login details in this way. Egg, however, does a good job of pooling multiple accounts in one place for its customers, while Equiniti is worth taking a look at if you have a portfolio of shares that you would like to manage all in one place.

Egg egg.co.uk
Equiniti shareview.co.uk

Shopping online

We are so used to shopping online that you probably wouldn't think of online retailers as being "cloud services" – they're simply websites where you buy stuff. But in the case of both Amazon and eBay, for example, when you set up an account with your own online inventory of items that you are selling and an easily accessible record of your purchasing history, they suddenly become very powerful and useful tools that you can access from anywhere. To find out more about making the most from these sites, pick up a copy of *The Rough Guide to Saving & Selling Online*.

One company that has made a big impact in terms of a fully featured cloud experience is Ocado, the online arm of Waitrose supermarket. Their iPhone app is particularly impressive, enabling you to easily complete your weekly shopping in around ten minutes whilst sat on the train heading to the office.

Amazon amazon.com (US) & amazon.co.uk (UK)

eBay ebay.com (US) & ebay.co.uk (UK)

Ocado ocado.co.uk (UK)

Online payment methods

Anyone who has used eBay will be familiar with PayPal, the company's online payment system. You can also use PayPal on many other sites and avoid the need to spread your credit card numbers and bank payment details around the web. Another useful payment scheme worth subscribing to is Google Checkout, which works similarly to PayPal, but has the additional advantage that it can be set to conceal your email address from online stores so that you don't end up adding to your junk email load every time you shop online.

PayPal paypal.com (US) & paypal.co.uk (UK)

Google Checkout checkout.google.com (UK & US)

Beware the phishermen

"Phishing" is a cunning form of online scam in which someone pretends to be from your bank, ISP or any other such body, and asks you to hand over your personal information either directly or via a webpage. The classic example is a scammer sending out a

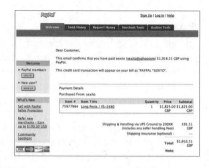

mass email claiming to be from a bank, with a link pointing to a webpage purportedly on a real bank's website. In fact, all the details are slightly incorrect (for example, the page might be at www.hsbc-banking.com instead of www.hsbc.com). But the recipient might not notice and assume the email is legitimate, following the instructions to "confirm" their online banking details on the fake site – in the process giving them to a criminal, who can then empty their account. The moral of the story is never to respond to emails – or instant messages – requesting private information, however legitimate the message might seem. Windows now comes with a phishing filter built in, but it still pays to be vigilant.

Be careful of "adult" sites

It is often said that the majority of online scams involve porn sites – the scammers believing, probably correctly, that the victims will be too embarrassed to report the problem. If you do ever use an adult site, never pass over your credit card details unless you're prepared to get stung. And, whatever you do, don't download any software they might offer.

Passwords

You probably already use a plethora of passwords and user IDs for the sites you frequently visit, and once you start investigating the sites within these pages you will have accumulated a whole lot more. Though obvious, there are a few basic ground rules worth reiterating here to make sure that your online identity remains secure – from online criminals, but also from members of your household who might inadvertently use your logins.

► **Make it "strong"** It really should go without saying that you shouldn't use the word "password" as a password. Neither should you opt for your pets' or family members' names. Instead, go for something with both letters and numbers, upper and lower case letters, and preferably one that makes no sense at all … something like "Gup345Pug".

► **Use User Accounts** Utilizing a User Account on your computer that requires a password at login (and also when your machine wakes from Sleep or exits Screen Saver mode) offers a very basic way to keep

Keychains & system security

Though beyond the scope of this book, it is worth understanding the way your computer saves passwords to a keychain and manages its own security and encryption. On a Windows 7 PC, acquaint yourself with the options within **Control Panel > User Accounts and Family Safety > Credential Manager**; on a Mac see what's on offer within **Applications > Utilities > Keychain Access**. For a more in-depth discussion, check out *The Rough Guide to Windows 7* and *The Rough Guide to Macs & OS X*.

all your domestic online activity ring-fenced and password protected. For more on User Accounts, turn to p.37.

► **Use multiple passwords** It's a good idea to create separate passwords for different logins on different sites. That way, if the password you use on one site is compromised, there is no danger that it can be used for any other sites. If this sounds like way too much to have to remember, come up with a secret formula – perhaps using the same basic root for all your passwords and then adding the initials of a given website's name.

► **Change them regularly** Again, this might sound like time that could be spent doing something less boring instead, but get into the habit of refreshing your passwords on a regular basis – perhaps make it a recurring monthly task on your Remember The Milk to-do list (see p.100).

Password managers

Another option for managing the myriad passwords you have now collected is a password manager. This is basically a piece of software that stores all your login details within an encrypted database on your computer ready for you to call upon them when your browser needs them.

Most browsers have such a feature built in. You can either set it up to automatically enter login details for you when you visit specific sites, or have it ask you for a master password to log in to any number of sites, so that you can keep your passwords private while only having to remember one password to rule them all. The latter strategy is always going to be better than simply using the feature as an automatic form-filler. Look for the options within your browser's Preferences or Settings screen to get started. In Firefox, for example, open **Preferences** and check the options under the **Security** tab.

Apart from the security that password managers offer within a busy household, one of the most important reasons to use one, even if you only use a few passwords, is that they can't be fooled by phishing websites (see p.64) masquerading as the real thing. They don't, however, generally work with the more complicated login details required by online banks – this kind of information is best kept inside your head, and in your head only, anyway.

There are also third-party password managers out there, which sell themselves on the premise that their encryption is stronger than that offered by browsers. Many also have mobile versions for cellphones and PDAs. A few worth checking out include:

1Password agilewebsolutions.com (Mac)
KeePass keepass.info (PC & Mac)
RoboForm roboform.com (PC)

Another alternative is to use a third-party authentication system such as that offered by OpenID (see p.160), although these are not universally recognized, and so may only work with certain sites that have signed up with the scheme.

Online resources

For more advice and information on online fraud and securing mobile devices, see:

CyberCrime cybercrime.gov
OnGuardOnline onguardonline.gov
Scambusters scambusters.com
Wikipedia en.wikipedia.org/wiki/internet_fraud
Info World: iPhone security tinyurl.com/ncglpu

Security on the road

Much of what has already been said in this chapter also applies when you are using computers other than your own, though it is definitely worth reiterating a few golden rules to help keep you and your data safe and secure away from home.

When using public machines

The most important thing to say here is that you need to cover your tracks. Whatever you are doing – checking email, using eBay, whatever – try to find a machine with a browser that you are familiar with. That way you will be able to reset the browser before you leave, making sure that none of your passwords or login details have been remembered. Many browsers, including recent versions of Safari, Internet Explorer and Firefox also feature a "private browsing" mode – once enabled you can surf and use your logins without the computer recording any cookies, history, password details or temporary internet files.

When using your laptop or netbook

Use a screen lock and password-protected login so that, should your machine be lost or stolen, its data will be inaccessible. If you use Wi-Fi hotspots, avoid accessing your bank accounts and any other sensitive material, as public networks are notorious for so-called "snoop" or "sidejacking" attacks where data is easily intercepted by other machines using the same network. Where possible limit your activities to browsing that isn't security-sensitive. And always try to disguise your keystrokes when entering passwords, just as you would with your PIN at an ATM. Finally, make sure you update your software regularly as a first line of defence against hacks.

When using a web-capable phone

As with laptops and netbooks, keep the phone's firmware and software up to date, cover your keys when entering login details, and *always* use a screen or keypad lock that kicks in after a minute or so to protect your data should your phone go walkabout. Many handsets also offer the option to auto-wipe all their data after a certain number of invalid attempts to unlock the keypad. If you have an iPhone and an Apple MobileMe account (see p.128) you can use the "Find my iPhone" feature (pictured below) to remotely track the location of your phone, add a four-digit passcode and even wipe all its content remotely.

In terms of browsers, it is worth treating your phone just as you would a public machine and making sure that it doesn't remember your passwords and login details by default as you browse. The same goes for any apps that require passwords.

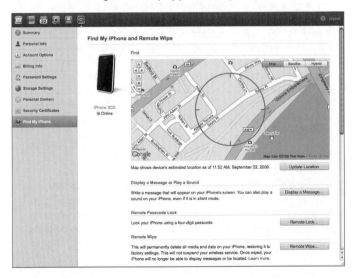

Backing up strategies

What with viruses, hardware crashes, computer thefts and other potential risks to your data, it's worth having some kind of backing-up strategy for everything that would be a pain to lose.

Local files

Anything stored locally (ie on your computer, not in the cloud) should be backed up fairly regularly onto some kind of removable media such as an external hard drive. Windows features a Backup Wizard which can help you set up a regular backup schedule to an external hard drive, while recent versions of Mac OS X come with a built-in application called Time Machine. Both can be used to back up all the data on your machine – your music, address book, bookmarks and mail included.

Cloud files

In theory, anything you keep online should be relatively safe from deletion. Any cloud service provider worth their salt will be making sure that all data that they host is well protected and adequately backed up should they ever suffer problems with any one of their servers. That said, you may still want to occasionally back up online resources yourself. A Gmail archive might be one online resource worth considering. The easiest way to do this is to enable POP within Gmail's Settings and then add your Gmail account to a "local" mail client (such as Mail on a Mac or Thunderbird on a PC). If you then regularly open the mail client on your computer it will effectively mirror your online archive (see below).

Mirroring files

Taking the mirroring idea a step further, services such as Apple's MobileMe subscription service and Microsoft's Windows Live services can be used to sync emails, bookmarks and contacts (see p.72) between your computers and your online account. These services turn up again and again throughout this book, and for more on some of the other means of staying "in sync" in this way, read the following chapter.

5

Staying in sync

Any time ... anywhere

At the heart of a productive and empowering digital lifestyle is syncing. What you will want is to have your contacts, calendars and emails available to you any time and anywhere. If you use one set of email and calendar tools with web access then you are probably more than happy. However, if you are one of the many people who use multiple email accounts, perhaps a work calendar and another calendar service at home, and are looking to have it all available on a mobile phone (or three), then you are going to have to think seriously about the way you synchronize all that material. Without going into the nuts and bolts of the process and dragging you through a series of arduous walk-throughs, this chapter looks at a few of the major syncing services and what they have to offer.

MobileMe

apple.com/mobileme

For Mac users who already have an iPhone, a MobileMe account can make a lot of sense. Yes, it requires you to pay an annual fee, but the syncing features are exceptionally smooth. MobileMe supports so-called "push" services, which means that when new emails reach the MobileMe servers they are instantly pushed through to any registered iPhones, any iPod touch connected to Wi-Fi, Apple Mail on your computer and also the me.com web app (see p.128). The same is true of contacts and calendars – when you edit a calendar or contact entry on your iPhone, say, the change is almost instantaneously reflected on the web app, as well as on any Macs and PCs registered to the MobileMe account. And it's all handled over the airwaves, so there's no need to connect your phone for the changes to take root on your other phones and computers.

MobileMe on a PC

Many Windows users settle for Microsoft's Windows Live and its sync features for shifting data to mobile devices. If you have an iPhone but still use a Windows PC, then you could consider MobileMe to handle things. The main difference is that Windows users need to download a special MobileMe Control Panel to handle sync options and iDisk settings. It can be found here: support.apple.com/downloads/MobileMe_Control_Panel_for_Windows.

More Mac syncing

Mac users additionally get to synchronize a hefty bundle of other pieces of data between multiple Macs. From **System Preferences > MobileMe > Sync** check the boxes next to the features you would like to synchronize – everything from Dock items and Notes to Widgets and System Preferences are made available for syncing.

As for synchronizing files and folders, MobileMe uses the iDisk feature to handle all that, which is discussed in more detail in this book's "Online Storage" chapter starting on p.117.

Google Sync Services

google.com/sync

The aforementioned MobileMe is pretty much a closed shop when it comes to options for synchronizing its data with other platforms and mobile phones (aside from the iPhone). Google, on the other hand, are up for the party and offer the means to sync with a plethora of mobile devices (including the iPhone and BlackBerry) and desktop applications (see below).

Though you could choose to spend all your time using Google's online Contacts and Calendars tools, you might run into problems if you ever need to access the data offline, which is why syncing with a desktop program is such a good idea.

Setting up a synchronization system is often a breeze, but at other times can be a real headache, especially when dealing with several systems or services. You will need to think seriously about exactly what you want the sync to achieve, so that you know which options to choose once you get started. Depending on how you use your different calendars and contact lists, you might want either a two-way sync (where changes made in both locations are reflected on the other), or a one-way sync (if you only ever make changes on one of the platforms).

Calendars

If you have already migrated your email accounts to Gmail (see p.82) it makes sense to synchronize your calendars too, so that everything is available to you in one place online. The Google Sync help pages offer advice for syncing Microsoft Outlook, Apple's iCal calendar application and Mozilla's Sunbird calendar app. Calendar syncing between desktop applications and Google

Calendars isn't always as straightforward as you might hope, and it's worth reading the list of "known issues" before making the choice to start syncing. Syncing Google Calendars to a mobile phone is, however, generally a pretty stress-free process.

Contact lists

As with using Calendars, building a nest for your contacts in the cloud can be very useful, and Google offers plenty of tools to get the job done – both in terms of synchronizing contacts from other desktop applications and also with regard to moving them over to your mobile device. As with Calendars, expect to come across a few anomalies (you might not be able to sync certain fields from your contacts' details or you may find that your sync generates duplicates); whatever problems you may encounter, you can be sure that someone else has had the same issue, and found a solution, so look online for help. There are also some useful articles here: google.com/support/contactsync.

Plaxo

plaxo.com

Plaxo is more than just an online address book, or calendar, it is a fully featured online community hub, for want of a better phrase, that lets you pool information and feeds from multiple sources, including Facebook, Bebo, Twitter and loads of others (for a similar service, also see FriendFeed, p.193); you can even integrate feeds from Last.fm (see p.168) and add your Amazon Wish Lists.

As for the question of synchronization, it's the Plaxo Address Book that offers an interesting twist. Whenever you edit the details of one of the contacts in your Address Book, anyone else

on Plaxo who has that individual's details in their address book also has them updated in their list. Synchronization can also be carried out between the Plaxo Address Book and Mozilla's Thunderbird, Google Contacts, Yahoo!, MSN Hotmail and Apple's OS X Address Book. You can additionally set things up for use with Microsoft Outlook, but only if you sign up for the premium Plaxo Pro version of the service, which isn't cheap at present. So, in theory, you could use Plaxo as a means of syncing all these different platforms in one fell swoop. The online Plaxo Address Book is also very easy to use and offers tools for managing duplicates and also backing everything up.

When you set up the synchronization for Windows, Mac OS X, Google or Yahoo!, you also pull across all calendar information to synchronize with the Plaxo Calendar.

In the past there have been questions raised about Plaxo pooling so much information – and, of course, the login details for several services – so in response the company has worked hard to reassure users that their data and passwords are safe on their servers.

More mobile sync options please

As better and better web-enabled phones come to market, and as more and more people become familiar with managing data synchronization, we can expect to see plenty more solutions coming over the horizon to ensure that all of our contacts, calendars, emails and data are with us all the time, everywhere we go.

A recent study into the current syncing options available (conducted by Funambol – themselves a provider of sync solutions) observed that the majority of services out there are free (MobileMe being the notable exception), and that mobile network providers tend to offer the least appealing offerings, while web-based services, and those offered by hardware manufacturers, have a lot more to shout about. As suggested by the path that Plaxo (see p.76) has taken, the report also identifies the syncing of social networking site data as an important upcoming theme and additionally mentions "wireless desktop integration" as an area that will also see growth very soon.

To read the complete report from Funambol, visit *funambol.com/solutions/library.php* and look for the link under the "White Papers" heading.

Part 2: Life in the cloud

6

Staying in touch

The second coming of webmail ... and beyond

Email and communication is probably the one area of cloud computing that you are already using without even knowing it. Over the last few years, millions of people across the world have been ditching their desktop email clients in favour of fast, versatile web-based mail tools. But this chapter looks at more than just email – communicating via the internet is also about chat, phone calls and even video calling. And that's even before you consider the mobile element.

Gmail

mail.google.com

The advantage of signing up with web-based email services is that they don't tie you to your internet provider. Furthermore, they provide so much online storage for your messages that you can leave all your emails permanently online (allowing you to access them from anywhere) as well as downloading them to an email program on your Mac or PC ("POP3 access").

At the time of writing there are many email choices out there, and the majority of them offer some kind of web access. Apple's MobileMe email service is a popular choice, as are the services provided by other big names such as Yahoo! and Microsoft. None, however, currently have the features of Google's free Gmail service, and there are few compelling reasons to go elsewhere.

What's more, Gmail can be used to send and receive messages for several different accounts and addresses (just as you might

Email jargon buster

Email can be collected and sent in various ways, the most common being POP, IMAP and Exchange. Here's the lowdown on each type:

▶ **POP** With a POP (or POP3) email account, messages can be sent and received via an email program, such as Mail (Mac) or Outlook (PC). Each time you check your mail, new messages are downloaded from your provider's mail server into your mail program. It's a bit like a real-world postal service – and, indeed, POP stands for Post Office Protocol. When using a computer and mail program in this way, messages are usually deleted from the server as you down-load them. Though it is possible to leave copies "in the cloud" so that you can download them to other computers and read them via web access, POP3 is really all about managing mail with desktop mail applications.

▶ **IMAP** An IMAP account can also send and receive via an email program, but all the messages are based in the cloud, not on your computer. If you do use a mail program with IMAP set up, it downloads the email headers (from, to, subject etc). Clicking on a message will download the full text of the message, but not delete it from the server. IMAP stands for Internet Message Access Protocol.

▶ **Exchange** Exchange is Microsoft's corporate system. If you use Outlook at work, it's likely that you're using an Exchange email account; and, assuming your administrator allows it, you can set up an Exchange account so that you can access it via the web, from home using a mail program, or from mobile or smart-phones that can handle Exchange.

▶ **Web access** Most POP, IMAP and Exchange email providers also let you send and receive email via a website. Everything resides in the cloud, and you read and compose your mail from within a web browser, from anywhere that you can get online. Gmail is designed for use via the web in this way.

with a regular mail application), which means you don't have to ditch old addresses and accounts that you are currently using – instead you simply pool them all in one place with Gmail.

On the downside, when you're viewing your messages via the web, you may have to view adverts on the page; there's no guarantee the service will remain free forever; and, if you have a common name, you may end up with an address as catchy as johnsmith2972@gmail.com.

Making the most of Gmail

To give a sense of why Gmail is almost certainly the best email system currently on offer, and to help you get the most from it if you've already signed up, here's a quick look at some of its best features.

▶ **Threaded emails** Gmail keeps your email organized automatically by combining all messages with the same subject line into "conversations". This makes it dramatically easier to stay on top of everything.

▶ **Archive and search** Once you've finished with an email or conversation, simply click the **Archive** button and the messages will be removed from your inbox to keep things tidy. You can still access all your old messages via the excellent search tool or by clicking **All Mail**.

▶ **Import and send email from other accounts** If you're switching from another email system such as Yahoo! or Hotmail, or from an ISP account, you can automatically pick up new messages from your old account, along with any messages stored on the server, by clicking **Settings > Accounts > Get mail from other accounts**. One of the best and most unusual features of Gmail is that it allows you not only to pick up email from other accounts, but also to send from other accounts. This means you can log in to one website to check and send from all your home, work and other email accounts. To set this up, click **Settings > Accounts** and specify the account you want to be able to send from.

▶ **Ads are optional** Many online email services oblige you to look at ads. With Gmail, however, all you see is a mix of small text ads and

Still want a mail program?

Though modern webmail services such as Gmail are great, for many people there's still no substitute for using a decent email application – or "client" – to compose, read, sort and organize email on a computer. The most obvious choice is the one already installed on your machine. Modern PCs and Macs both come with a program simply called Mail. These share the same name but are completely unrelated. Both are pretty good, with all the features required by the typical email user.

As for alternatives, the most popular free email client is Thunderbird, a powerful open-source application for PC and Mac users. By far the most widely used paid-for client is Outlook, which ships as part of Microsoft Office for PC. The Mac version is called Entourage, but it's essentially the same program. It's certainly worth giving Outlook or Entourage a try if you have Office, but otherwise they're not worth shelling out for.

There are also third-party applications available that give Gmail the look and feel of a desktop program. On a Mac try MailPlane or, alternatively, use an application called Fluid, which can create a custom desktop program from pretty much any webpage. Also worth looking at is a program called GeeMail, which works with PCs, Macs and also Linux machines.

Thunderbird mozilla.org/products/thunderbird
Outlook microsoft.com/outlook
Entourage mactopia.com
MailPlane mailplaneapp.com
Fluid fluidapp.com
GeeMail sourcebits.com/geemail

Mailplane
Brings Gmail to your Mac desktop

mixed news headlines above your inbox. If you don't like these, you can simply turn them off by clicking **Settings > Web Clips**.

▶ **Huge amount of storage space** At the time of writing, Gmail offers around seven gigabytes of storage space for each account, and this rises over time. You can see at a glance how much space you've used up at the bottom of the screen.

▶ **Labs** Click **Settings > Labs** to reveal a huge range of extra features that are currently being developed either by Google themselves or by other programmers. You'll find lots of useful things in there. At the time of writing, the best picks on offer include a Task list (see p.105), and an option for automatically archiving emails as you reply to them – really handy for keeping your inbox tidy.

▶ **Firefox add-ons** If you use Gmail in Firefox you also get to take advantage of many available add-ons that broaden the browser's functionality. The Better Gmail 2 add-on (addons.mozilla.org/en-US/firefox/addon/6076) offers some great additions to Gmail, including an unread message icon on your browser tab.

More from Google...

At the time of writing, Google has some very exciting new communications projects coming through. Google Voice will give you one special Google phone number that can be used to manage all your other numbers. Various screening, voicemail and conferencing features are also promised. Google Voice will initially be US-only, but keep an eye out for the global roll-out.

Google Wave, meanwhile, looks set to revolutionize the way people communicate and collaborate online and pulls together many features of the current Google suite (such as the collaborative element of Google Docs) but with some very interesting twists.

Google Voice voice.google.com
Google Wave wave.google.com

Skype

skype.com

Skype is what's known as a VoIP (Voice over Internet Protocol) client; in other words, it makes phone calls via the internet as opposed to the traditional means used by the phone companies. Assuming you have broadband, you can use a Skype account to make free computer-to-computer calls – with or without video – to anyone, anywhere in the world, who also has a Skype account. You can also pay to call regular landlines and mobile phones. This can be very useful if your home phone is often in use, effectively providing a second line without any standing charge. Potentially, it can also slash your phone bills, especially if you regularly call long distance.

There are even mobile Skype apps available for various handset platforms (the iPhone app is pictured to the left), though mobile network providers are understandably reluctant to let Skype traffic use their data networks, so expect only to use such apps over a Wi-Fi network.

Skype also gives you a means of instant messaging from both the desktop and mobile versions, in the same way that you can with the other messaging clients discussed overleaf.

Meebo

meebo.com

Back in the internet days of old, "chat" referred to geeky Internet Relay Chat, complete with its obscure commands, confusing channels and free-for-all chat rooms, which were mainly used by frustrated teenagers (plus the occasional pervert) to flirt with each other. Thankfully, things have moved on. Today, "chat" programs let you exchange real-time typed messages with friends and family – and also make voice and video calls. Such programs offer a fun way to communicate and can save you money, too. Of the web-based chat clients out there, Meebo is the best one to get started with as it supports login details from most of the main chat networks and online community platforms (including Yahoo!, Facebook Chat, AIM, ICQ, MySpaceIM, Google Talk and Jabber).

There are also mobile versions of Meebo and a special Firefox extension; and best of all, it's free to use.

Beejive

beejive.com

As for mobile messaging, most of the main networks and clients have been busily pushing out mobile apps in recent years. The AIM iPhone app, for example, was among the very first apps to ever appear in the iTunes App Store, and dozens have followed in its wake.

Arguably the best of the bunch is Beejive, a mobile instant messenger app available for the BlackBerry, iPhone and also devices running Windows Mobile. It can be used to chat on AIM, iChat, MobileMe, MSN, Yahoo!, MySpaceIM, Google Talk, ICQ, Jabber, and, additionally on the iPhone, Facebook Chat. Where Beejive really comes into its own is as a free replacement for SMS text messaging; and thanks to push notifications, your friends will see that they have received a message on their phone, even when they don't have the app running.

chapter 6

Staying in touch with the day's events

One of the greatest things to happen to the web in recent years has been the massive growth of RSS – short for Really Simple Syndication. RSS allows you to view "feeds" (or "newsfeeds") from blogs, news services and other websites. Each feed consists of headlines of new or updated articles, along with the full text or a summary or extract. If you see something that you'd like to read, click on the headline to view the full story.

There are numerous ways to read RSS feeds (through email clients, stand-alone programs, etc), but if you want all your feeds to hover in the cloud, and be available to you from any machine with an internet connection, then you will need to use a web-based RSS aggregator such

as Google Reader (*reader.google.com*). If you already have a Google account, then look for the link at the top of your Gmail page to get started.

Though you can access a mobile version of Google Reader from any phone with a web browser via the address listed above, a dedicated RSS app is going to give a better experience. iPhone users should check out the excellent Net News Wire app (*newsgator.com/individuals/netnewswireiphone*), while those with a BlackBerry should hook up with Viigo (*viigo.com*).

7

Contacts
& calendars

Cloud-based tools that show you who, where and when

This isn't the type of book that most people will read from cover to cover, but if you are doing so, you will have already read the chapter on "Staying in sync" (see p.71). That chapter offered a few clues as to who the big names are in online contact and calendar suites, and there are no prizes for guessing that we are talking about the likes of Microsoft, Apple, Yahoo! and Google. This chapter takes a look at the tools they have on offer and also mentions a few other possibilities worth exploring.

Google Calendar

calendars.google.com

There is nothing worse than an unresponsive, slow-to-load and glitchy web app (see MobileMe on p.94). Thankfully, Google Calendar falls into none of these categories. It's very easy to get the hang of and has an excellent search feature for quickly tracking down appointments by keyword. As well as the regular calendar views there is a very useful "Agenda" view, which displays all your appointments as a scrollable chronological list.

By digging around in **Settings > Labs** you can also add a few extras to the mix, including the ability to add Google Docs attachments to events and also a "Next Meeting" option, which when enabled gives you a handy panel dedicated to what's coming up next.

Google Contacts

contacts.google.com

Google Contacts does everything you would expect it to do: for example, you can add and edit contacts, and associate photos with individual entries, just as you might with the desktop client you use on your Mac or PC.

Where it gets clever is the way it integrates with the rest of your Google suite of tools, which, remember, are all accessed using the same Google account details. Aside from being able to view your contacts from the link listed at the top of this page, you can also view and manage your contacts from within Gmail – there's a link in the left-hand sidebar (as pictured below). Other useful features of Google Contacts include the ability to click straight through from an address to a Google Map of the location and the fact that whenever you send an email to someone new, they are automatically added to your contacts database.

Also worth noting is the integration with Google Docs (see p.138): when you want to share documents with others, your contacts list is only a click away, making the whole process far easier than messing around with email attachments.

MobileMe Calendar

me.com/calendar

Apple's subscription service MobileMe – previously monikered .Mac (pronounced *dot Mac*) – has received very mixed reviews over the years. Aside from the fact that it's paid for, when services from several other companies come free, the most common criticism to be levelled at MobileMe is that its web-based apps leave a lot to be desired. The browser-based calendar, for example, can be painfully slow to load, while creating new events can be fiddly and frustrating. And yet there is still something very pleasing about the interface as a whole, especially the way all your MobileMe tools rack up alongside each other. No doubt it is this extra gloss and the impressive graphics that slow the overall experience, so one assumes that Apple are working on the principle that when hardware and internet speeds catch up, their suite is going to float to the top of the pond.

MobileMe Contacts

me.com/contacts

Though not as glitchy as the Calendar tool described opposite, Apple's web-based Contacts organizer is similarly slow on occasion, and yet equally well-designed. What's more, the tools for creating new contacts (illustrated below) are feature-rich and make the job easy. Perhaps most importantly, however – and this also goes for the MobileMe Calendars – the way that MobileMe syncs with both Mac OS X and the Apple iPhone is impressively smooth. So, what's the bottom line for MobileMe Contacts and Calendars? Well, if you already use Apple Mac computers and have an iPhone then you may well conclude that it's worth paying for the service. If, on the other hand, you are looking to integrate your digital life with several different platforms, non-Apple phones and numerous other online PIM (Personal Information Manager) services, you are probably better off saving your money.

Yahoo! Calendar

calendar.yahoo.com

Yahoo!'s Calendar tool remains one of the most widely used on the web, despite the prominent banner ads that haunt its interface. The online tool itself is pretty strong, with a quick-to-load tab-based system for different calendar views, various options for syncing with mobile devices and a means of sharing schedules and calendars with other Yahoo! Calendar users.

If you are a Yahoo! Mail user already then it's a pretty compelling offering and is easily accessed via a link on the left-hand panel of the Yahoo! Mail screen.

Event scheduling in the cloud

One problem to be overcome with some online calendar systems is how to schedule events and meetings for multiple people, who may well all use different calendar services. One solution is to use Doodle – a free web-based scheduling tool that can be used to create a shortlist of proposed dates, which recipients then get to cast their vote against. It's simple but effective and it works with Microsoft Outlook, Google Calendar and Apple iCal. Find out more at doodle.com.

Windows Live Calendar

windowslive.com/online/calendar

Microsoft's suite of online tools (which these days all nestle
under the banner of Windows Live) have upped their game
considerably in recent years. Anyone familiar with the Windows
Calendar desktop application will have no problems adjusting to
using this sleek browser-based offering, and the way it integrates
with Windows Live Hotmail is useful enough, though not earth-
shattering in its ingenuity. Never one to keep things simple,
Microsoft offers you three ways to share your calendars using the
Windows Live Calendar tools:

▶ **Private sharing** Specified friends can be invited to use their
Windows Live ID to edit events within a given calendar.

▶ **View-only sharing** This allows others to subscribe to a given
calendar and view it, but not make any changes to it.

▶ **Public sharing** This allows other people to search for a given
calendar and view it on the web, whoever they are.

Cozi

cozi.com

This web-based tool is an all-singing-and-dancing family organization portal – think of it as a replacement for all those pieces of paper stuck on the refrigerator or lost at the bottom of your twelve-year-old's gym bag. Alongside shopping lists, journalling pages and a family messaging tool, the real selling point is the family calendar, which can sync with Outlook on a Windows PC and offers colour coding for each member of the family. As well as the online browser version, there is a handy Windows Gadget and mobile versions of Cozi are available for the iPhone, Windows smartphones and also some newer BlackBerrys. Cozi works in the UK, the US and many other territories, but certain SMS features are currently only available in the US. As for the cost, it's free to use, but expect a certain amount of targeted marketing in exchange for the privilege.

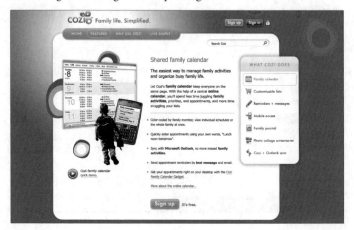

8

To-do lists

You'll never be able to say "I forgot" again

O nce you start using to-do lists, you'll wonder how you ever managed without one. Much more functional than a piece of paper that you keep in your back pocket (and less likely to get put through the washing machine), online to-do lists are eminently flexible and really can take on the role of a virtual personal assistant. Assuming, that is, you pick one that actually makes you more productive, rather than one that is so fiddly to use that it does the exact opposite. This chapter looks at the services worth considering.

Remember The Milk

rememberthemilk.com

File under "probably-the-best-productivity-tool-out-there-right-now-and-certainly-the-one-with-the-coolest-icon". With over 800,000 users, Remember The Milk (RTM) is among the most popular task managers to be found online … and that's no accident.

Far more than just a basic list and check-box system, it allows you to produce multiple lists (for Work, Home, Study, etc) and add as much or as little detail as you need. You can even associate tasks with specific geographical locations and then integrate those locations with Google Maps. More importantly, RTM allows you to postpone and edit your tasks not only from within the website, but also from numerous mobile apps (see box opposite), browser plug-ins and Widgets: it's this seamless synchronization that both makes the service so useful and earns it its "cloud computing" stripes. Here are a couple more of its most appealing features:

▶ Firefox sidebar integration

Use the link rememberthemilk.com/services/modules/googleig to view a streamlined version of your to-do list in Firefox. Bookmark the page, then choose **Bookmarks > Organize Bookmarks** and highlight the bookmark you just created. Finally, check the **Load this Bookmark in the sidebar** box to make it a permanent resident on the left-hand side of your Firefox browser.

▶ **Gmail integration** It is similarly easy to add RTM to the left-hand panel of Gmail. Use either the appropriate Firefox extension or the slick little Gadget from Google Labs. For the lowdown on both, visit: rememberthemilk.com/services/gmail.

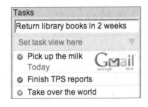

▶ **Email posting** You can create new tasks via a special email address; this is a really useful means of filing away items from your regular email inbox that you might want to come back to at a particular time.

▶ **Jott posting** In the US and Canada you can also add tasks by simply calling 1-866-JOTT-123, thanks to this Jott.com mash-up.

▶ **Twitter posting** Add RTM as a friend on Twitter and then access your tasks via direct messaging. Find out more at rememberthemilk.com/services/twitter.

The basic version of the RTM service is free, but there is also a Pro account that will set you back $25 a year. You will need to go with the latter to be able to use the apps mentioned in the box below, though it's money well spent in this writer's opinion.

Remember The Milk, out and about

The simplest way to get at your Remember The Milk task lists using any mobile device with a browser is via the *m.rememberthemilk.com* web app, which is light on features, but does the job and is quick to load. There are also various mobile apps available to download and install, including RTM for Android, MilkSync for Windows Mobile and BlackBerry devices, and also a very good iPhone/iPod touch app that features badge icon and push notification support. For more on all the available RTM access options, visit: *rememberthemilk.com/services*.

Todoist

todoist.com

In contrast to Remember The Milk (see p.100), Todoist's
presentation of tasks is based around a left-hand sidebar of task
categories, which work a bit like Gmail's Labels system. This
makes for a very clear, and colourful, interface. To its credit, the
site is very flexible in the ways that it can be used: it's easy to set
up hierarchies of "sub-projects" and "sub-items" so that it becomes
more of a project management tool than a basic to-do list.

As for third-party integration, it slots nicely into Gmail and
can be used, like Remember The Milk, in the Firefox sidebar;
there are also Netvibes and iGoogle widgets available for
download. Unfortunately, the Todoist mobile offerings are pretty
unimpressive at the time of writing, so it's worth checking what
they have for your handset before diving in.

Ta-da List

tadalist.com

If you want a very basic but well-designed to-do list, then this is the one to go for. It might be spartan, but it gets the job done, and is far easier to read than some of the more complex offerings.

The same company also offers a web-based project management tool called Basecamp (basecamphq.com), which integrates a more fully featured version of the Ta-da List tool into a suite of blogging, scheduling and file-sharing tools. It is largely aimed at firms (even the basic version will cost you $24 each month), but if you have a small business it might be just what you are looking for.

The basic, standalone version of Ta-da List, meanwhile, is completely free to use and can also be accessed via a very good iPhone web app (point your iPhone's browser at tadalist.com and it automatically loads the iPhone version).

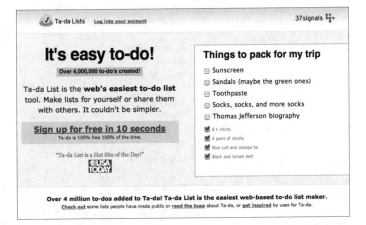

Toodledo

toodledo.com

Another very versatile to-do list platform, Toodledo, in the company's own words, offers "...folders, subtasks, due dates, priorities, tags, contexts, goals, notes, time estimates and other information to easily organize, search and sort

through your tasks". In addition to the free version, there is also the option to sign up for "Pro" ($14.95 per year) and "Pro Plus" ($29.95 per year) accounts, both of which come bundled with a few extras, but nothing that would inspire the majority of users to

fork out the extra cash. The most significant enhancements include data encryption (which you probably won't need for the average shopping list) and being able to upload files and attach them to specific tasks (for Pro Plus account holders only).

Even if you just stick with the basic version, if you own an iPhone then the Toodledo app (pictured right) is worth shelling out a couple of dollars for via the iTunes App Store.

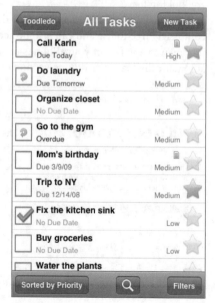

Google Tasks

google.com/calendar

If you already use Google Calendar to organize your
appointments, then you might decide that its built-in Tasks feature
is going to do the job just fine. Though it lacks the polish of
several of the dedicated services, its primary virtue is the fact that
it nestles within the Google suite, making it pretty hard to avoid
if you are a regular Google user – tasks appear next to the main
calendar, and those with an associated due date also appear within
the main calendar frame. If you don't see Tasks by default, hit
Settings and check the **Tasks** box.

Google Tasks can also be accessed via the iPhone Google app,
mobile web browsers (at gmail.com/tasks) and also via a handy
Tasks iGoogle Gadget (see p.129).

And finally, don't forget...

There are loads of to-do list apps out there, and many online webmail services and ISP portals also offer their own version of what is, really, a pretty basic concept. Here are a few more B-list possibilities if you don't happen to get on with those already listed:

► **ReminderFox** reminderfox.mozdev.org

► **Voo2do** voo2do.com

► **Yahoo! widget** widgets.yahoo.com/widgets/todo-list

► **Zirr.us** zirr.us

► **Zoho Planner** zohoplanner.com

9

Social bookmarks

Sharing the web...

Bookmarks (or "Favorites") are links to websites or pages that you might want to come back to at a later date. Traditionally, they have been locked away within your computer's browser, but they have now evolved to become a powerful, entertaining and useful way to enjoy the world wide web. The idea of social bookmarking is exactly that – you find a page you like and publish its address for the world to enjoy too. And as soon as you start pooling all your bookmarks in the cloud, they are additionally accessible to you anywhere that you can get online, and from any web-capable device.

StumbleUpon

stumbleupon.com

StumbleUpon has been passed around a bit. At one time it looked as if it would be bought by Google, and then eBay stepped up and purchased the company. It is now once again owned by its two founders, who bought it back in 2009 with the help of a few investors.

With a StumbleUpon account set up, you become part of a vast online community (the site's homepage claims over eight million users worldwide). Each of those members has their own homepage where they display all their favourite pages and links as thumbnails. From there it is up to you to click through and take a look at the page. At this point, even though you have navigated to another site, the StumbleUpon web toolbar (pictured below) stays glued to the top of your browser, allowing you to give the site you are looking at either a "thumbs up" if you like it or a "thumbs down" if you don't.

Though this may all seem a little frivolous, the really clever bit about StumbleUpon is that the more you use the toolbar to vote on pages, the better the site's "personalized recommendation engine" gets at predicting the kind of sites you might be interested in. And that's where the **Stumble!** button on the far left-hand end of the toolbar comes into play – click this and you are taken to what might at first appear to be a random webpage, but is in fact one based on a combination of your personal voting preferences, the preferences of the community as a whole, and also the choices you can make about "What interests you?" on your profile homepage. So the sites that you are presented with might be those that received plenty of "thumbs up" votes across the whole community as well as a positive response from users with similar interests to yours. You can also influence the results you get by building your own network of other users (you end up with a list of Stumbler "Friends", in the same way that you might maintain a "Friends" list on MySpace or Facebook).

But be warned, that Stumble! button can get very addictive and lead you off on all manner of tangents – and though you might find it entertaining, your boss probably won't share your enthusiasm.

Xmarks

xmarks.com

Without doubt one of the most useful tools featured in this
book, Xmarks performs the invaluable task of synchronizing
your "Bookmarks" and "Favorites" across multiple browsers and
multiple machines, including both Macs and Windows PCs. On
top of that, it also creates a personalized webpage of all your links
(complete with any folder structure you might use to organize
them) that can be accessed from anywhere that you can get
online. Integration is slightly different depending on whether you
are using Firefox, Internet Explorer or Safari (the Safari Xmarks
badge is pictured below), but in each case it simply and effortlessly
works, leaving you free to worry about everything else in your life,
safe in the knowledge that all your bookmarks are safely backed
up and in sync.

If you need more, then Xmarks will also provide you with
website recommendations based on your personalized interests
and the aggregated sites
from across the Xmarks
community – in short, sites
that have been bookmarked
the most frequently. With
Xmarks installed you'll
also see a change in your
Google searches, with
Xmarks-recommended
search results earning an
orange icon badge on your
search results page.

Digg

digg.com

Like the other sites listed in this chapter, Digg is all about community. In this instance, Digg members submit webpages and news stories that they are interested in, and everyone else gets to vote on whether they want to see the submission rise or fall in the Digg rankings – a process of either "digging" or "burying". The main criticism to be levelled at the community is that the resulting rankings tend to favour a mix of tech gossip and US-centric, slightly "laddish" news stories; but hey, if you want to be among the first to know about the latest must-have customization for your Linux netbook, or are perhaps interested in knowing who the ten "dumbest" characters were in the expanded *Star Wars* universe, then you may well find just what you are looking for.

Digg integrates well with Facebook, and there are various mobile apps that will dish up doses of Digg for you, but arguably the best way to passively consume the highest-ranking stories is via an RSS feed (there's a link for it on the homepage).

Reddit

reddit.com

Much like Digg (see the previous page), Reddit is a web-based, community-led links aggregator. Users post links to news stories and articles which are then voted up and down the rankings by the rest of the community. You also get to customize which categories you see on the site's homepage, and there are various mobile versions available for use when out and about. Again, like Digg, the content can be quite US-centric, but the site has a slightly friendlier feel to it (which might possibly be attributed to the grinning website logo and the fact that in exchange for high-scoring posts, users receive "karma" points).

Delicious

delicious.com

In the same style as other sites, the Delicious homepage features a "what's hot" list of the newest links and bookmarks to have been submitted by members of the community. The site's unique selling point, however, is the way you can manage and present the archive of bookmarks via keywords, or tags. Say, for example, you want to see all links about sausages, simply use the URL delicious.com/tag/sausages. As for its "cloud" credentials, you can upload and save all your own personal bookmarks to your account and then choose whether to make them public or keep them to yourself to access from anywhere that you can get online.

Google Bookmarks

google.com/bookmarks

As you might expect, Google have an offering in this realm.
Google Bookmarks is a service that allows you to pool bookmarks
in the cloud, add annotations and notes and access your
bookmarks from any machine – so you can bookmark something
in the office and then access the same URL when you get home.

Unlike the other services covered in this chapter, Google
Bookmarks are private, so you'll have to log into your Google
account to get at them. They do, however, incorporate a very
useful search feature that allows you to trawl not only the URLs
and page titles, but also all the content of each webpage when
searching for a specific bookmark – very useful when calling
to arms a bunch of bookmarks collected while researching a
particular subject.

A better Google search

One interesting side effect of using Google Bookmarks is that they will
influence the results of your Google searches from browsers where
you are logged into your Google account. Basically, the Google search
engine forms an idea of your interests by extrapolating from your bookmark history and uses that data to skew the results of your searches.
In theory, the more bookmarks you stockpile, the more relevant your
results should become. That said, you might find that you prefer your
Google searches without the distortion.

GMarks

If you use Firefox and Google Bookmarks, then it's worth installing the excellent GMarks extension (click **Tools > Add-ons** and then search for **GMarks**). GMarks displays your bookmarks in the Firefox sidebar and incorporates various tools to customize the display; it also boasts a really usable search function. If you need any extra help with GMarks, you can contact the developer direct via the GMarks Google Group (*groups.google.com/group/GMarks*).

If you use either Firefox or Internet Explorer (turn to p.16 to find out more about both), the best way to get started is to download the Google Toolbar (toolbar.google.com). Once installed, click the spanner-shaped icon, then **Toolbar Options > Tools**; check the **Bookmarks** checkbox and hit **Save**.

Next copy across your browser's bookmarks by clicking the bookmarks icon and then selecting the **Import bookmarks** option from the drop-down menu. You can then add new bookmarks by clicking the blue star icon; click a second time to add labels (which work similarly to those in Gmail). You can also add bookmarks from any browser using a special "bookmarklet", available from the address at the top of the previous page. This address is also the place to find your Google Bookmarks on the web.

There's additionally an iGoogle Gadget that can be used on your iGoogle homepage (see p.129). It displays all your bookmarks along with their labels; you can also edit them directly in the Gadget. A useful technique here is to add the Gadget to your page multiple times and create custom bookmark views in each for different categories and labels.

Twine

twine.com

Twine has a slightly more serious agenda than many of the social bookmarking sites. In fact, more than just a bookmarking community, the website is designed to create expanding discussions and comment forums around articles, posts and bookmarks. The bottom line is that it can be an incredibly useful research tool that really helps you target specific topics and have meaningful discussions with people who share your interests.

There is also a lot to be said for the design and layout of the site and its tools, which are infinitely easier to use than those of similar portals. This one is well worth trying out.

10

Online storage

Syncing files and folders to the cloud

This book has a whole chapter (see p.71) dedicated to keeping your personal information in sync – your emails, contacts and calendars. But if you really want to liberate your digital life, you also need to make your important documents, files and folders available anywhere that you can get connected to the internet. You could, of course, just rent some webspace somewhere and transfer your files there manually. But that's a cumbersome solution, and there are plenty of much tidier options out there. This chapter describes the best ones.

iDisk

me.com/idisk

Available as part of Apple's subscription MobileMe offering, the iDisk is generally regarded as being worth the price of the overall package on its own.

If you are a Mac user, with a MobileMe account set up, your iDisk can be activated within OS X from **System Preferences > MobileMe > iDisk**. This creates a new "drive" icon on your desktop where you can store whatever files you want. Everything within the iDisk is then synced with a cloud version of the same files, accessed from the web app version of your iDisk that's integrated into the me.com MobileMe suite (see p.128). In turn your iDisk can be synced with other Macs as well, meaning that you can be working on a particular file in the office and by the time you get home at the end of the day you will find that latest version of the file has reached your desktop computer before you.

This is all well and good, and is a great way to keep multiple Macs in sync and make sure that key files are backed up. But you don't have to use the Mac-based version of the tool at all if you don't want to. The iDisk web app, of course, can be used with any browser, using a Mac or PC, as a means of storing files. At the time of writing, a MobileMe account comes with 20GB of storage space by default, though you can upgrade and buy more if you need it. The interface is very good, and both uploading and downloading files is very intuitive. In addition, there is a very good, free iDisk app available from the iTunes App Store for reaching your files from either an iPhone or iPod touch.

Sharing files from an iDisk

One of the most useful functions of the iDisk is as a means of sharing files too large to email as attachments. You can either place them in the iDisk's "Public" folder (which can be accessed by anyone using the address public.me.com/youraccountname), or set up specific sharing parameters for individual files using the **Share** button alongside each file in the iDisk web app. You can set up a password for the file, set how long it is available to be shared and then send an email message to the people you want to share it with, complete with a link to download the file.

Other ways to share files

If you don't want to use MobileMe's iDisk as a means of sharing big files there are plenty of other alternative web services that avoid the perils of sending large files as email attachments. You can generally get away with sending a certain number of files for free, but expect to be hassled to sign up for a "Pro" account for more frequent use and larger file sizes. These are among the best-known services:

MailBigFile mailbigfile.com
RapidShare rapidshare.com
YouSendIt yousendit.com

Live Mesh

mesh.com

Microsoft has two offerings in the world of data storage. The first is SkyDrive (skydrive.live.com), which gives access to 25GB of online data storage to anyone with a Windows Live ID. The more interesting tool, however, is Live Mesh. With a maximum of 5GB to play with, you can specify which files on your Windows PC to sync with a cloud version, accessed from the Windows Live Home webpage (see p.132). From there you can sync the same files to more PCs, Macs and also mobile devices.

Sharing files is also possible; it's controlled via a special sidebar (the Mesh Bar), where you can specify who has access to your files and change your sync settings. The Windows desktop version of the Mesh Bar also features tools for communicating directly with friends using Windows Live Messenger.

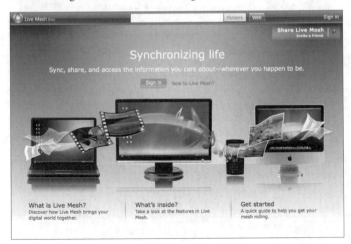

SugarSync

sugarsync.com

This well-respected online data-storage and sync service now offers a free account with 2GB of cloud-based storage space. There are also several services that give you much more space to play with in exchange for either a monthly or annual premium. The software runs on both Macs and PCs, and there are also mobile apps available for iPhones, BlackBerrys, Windows Mobile devices and phones running Android.

As with the other services that are worth looking at, SugarSync files can be accessed from anywhere via a web browser, and SugarSync provides tools for sharing files with others.

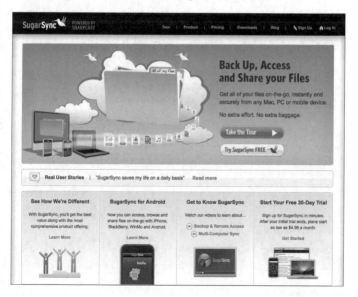

Viewing your home machine

If access to files is what you are after, then copying them to a third party's servers is not the only option. You might instead choose to simply leave them where they are and make them available remotely, over the internet.

There are various techie methods and protocols that can be employed to turn your computer into a "server" that's visible across the web – they are way beyond the scope of this book. Thankfully, there are also several services that will do the job for you without the headache of having to research and set it up yourself. Many perform the double whammy of giving you access to your computer's files (just as if they were on a hard drive connected directly) while also showing your home computer's desktop and giving you the power to control the machine from anywhere around the globe.

All these services work well, but they are at the mercy of the network connections that run between them, so expect a certain amount of hassle before you get them working just the way you want them to. Where possible, try to use them over wired networks as opposed to wireless networks – their performance will be far superior.

► **Back to My Mac**

apple.com/mobileme
Available as part of
Apple's MobileMe service, Back to My Mac
gives OS X Leopard and
OS X Snow Leopard
users remote access for
file sharing and screen
sharing between multiple

machines registered to the same MobileMe account. Look for the options within **System Preferences > MobileMe** (pictured).

► **GoToMyPC** *gotomypc.com* Though there is no off-the-peg free version of this service, signing up to the annual plan earns users a 25 percent discount on

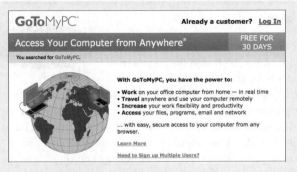

the normal monthly rates and there is a 30-day trial period that should give you an idea of what you'll get. It's a feature-packed service, with strong encrypted security, multiple-machine syncing functions and mobile access from Windows Mobile and Windows CE devices. As the name suggests, GoToMyPC works with Windows PCs, but not with Macs.

► **Live Mesh Remote Desktop** *mesh.com* Microsoft's Live Mesh (see p.120) bundles in a Remote Desktop tool. It enables you to access any machine within your "mesh" and can be used not only to get at files that have already been synchronized, but all files and folders on the machine. Though some Live Mesh services can be used with both Macs and PCs, this one is just for Windows machines.

► **LogMeIn** *LogMeIn.com* This company provides various services with different pricing models. LogMeIn Free is the one to kick off with and gives you remote access to your computer's desktop over the internet, along with file management controls and also use of printers connected to your home machine – meaning you could use it to send messages home, fax-style.

For an interesting twist on the idea of accessing your computer remotely, check out Simplify Media (see p.172), which gives you access to your iTunes music library over the internet from both remote computers and some mobile devices.

Wuala

wuala.com

Better known for manufacturing external hard drives, LaCie are also the company behind Wuala, an online data storage service. You start off with 1GB for free, and from there you can either purchase extra online capacity, or actually trade your own local disk space for its equivalent online. It sounds bizarre, but is actually very clever. By releasing some of your computer's drive to become part of the overall system, you are contributing to the power and capacity of the Wuala network as a whole.

But before you ask, this does not mean that you have someone else's files living on your machine. Well, not exactly. Every file uploaded to Wuala is split into tiny encrypted fragments that are distributed and backed up across the network. So any Wuala data that resides on your machine will be meaningless to you, and any of your data on other people's machines will be meaningless to them. And because your data is duplicated across multiple locations, even if a single machine containing one of your fragments goes offline, you can still access your file in its entirety. Clever, isn't it?

To get started, you need to download the Wuala software from their website – it's available for Windows, Mac and Linux machines. And to start trading your local storage capacity you need to make your computer available online for at least four hours a day. The more capacity you give, and the more hours you allow your computer to remain connected, the more online space you are entitled to.

Part 3: Work in the cloud

11

Online desktops

Your cloud computing home from home

This chapter takes a look at two very distinct things.
Firstly, it investigates the web-based tools that emulate
the computing environment you are used to: they give you
a desktop and apps to play with, and try hard to be a whole
operating system within a browser. Secondly, there are
the online desktops that aim to make the best use of your
browser's homepage. They aggregate the things you might need
all in one place – news, email, calendar reminders – using either
fully fledged web apps or more disposable and interchangeable
Gadgets and Widgets.

MobileMe Desktop

me.com

Many MobileMe account users set "me.com" as their browser homepage. From there, you are just a click away from the service's web apps for Mail, Contacts (see p.95), Calendar (see p.94), Gallery (see p.183), iDisk (see p.118) and Account Settings. Each has their own icon on the dark strip at the top of the interface (pictured below), making it quick and easy to switch between the various tools. As has been mentioned elsewhere, MobileMe web apps can be slow to load, but this will no doubt get better over time. Overall, this is a well-designed cloud suite and, for MobileMe users, a convenient place to end up when you open your browser.

iGoogle

google.com/ig

Much like the desktop Gadgets found in recent versions of
Windows, Google's iGoogle personalized homepages use Gadgets
to dish up everything from news, weather and maps, to eBay
watch lists, stock market news and RSS feeds.

An iGoogle homepage is free to use with a Google account
and can be manipulated into an infinite number of configurations,
depending on which Widgets you deploy. To see what's available,
click the **Add stuff** link and, for a really homely touch, change the
page's header strip by clicking **Change theme**.

Pageflakes

pageflakes.com

Another free-to-use customizable homepage tool, Pageflakes is very flexible and easy to use. All the individual "flakes", as they call them, can be dragged and dropped and there are loads to choose from. The way that the tool implements RSS feeds means that everything you get is always bang up to date – even if you never used it for anything else, Pageflakes is a great place to view all your feeds alongside each other. Compared to the alternatives, Pageflakes gives the most options for collaborating and sharing, and would make a great noticeboard for a small club or society.

Netvibes

netvibes.com

Like iGoogle, Netvibes gives you a customizable blank canvas to decorate with Widgets of your choice. This particular site's unique selling point, however, is a tab system that can be used to flip between different views, with categories such as "News", "Shopping", "Fun & Games", etc. Its integration of third-party email feeds is very smooth and the RSS support is excellent – especially handy if you are into podcasts, as you can play them directly from the page via a special audio Widget.

As with other sites, themes are on offer to change the overall appearance. It's free to set up and use, and you also get to create a "public page", to share with the world.

Windows Live Home

home.live.com

As a member of the Windows Live community you get a handy "jump-in" page that gives you a way into all your other Windows Live services. Your Windows email, community notifications and the current weather (what's wrong with looking out the window?) are all prominently displayed, and the page's colourful upper strip can be customized using the provided themes and by adding your own uploaded pictures. Clicking the **Web activities** button allows you to create links to other sites and services and integrate them into your Windows Live pages; all the usual suspects are on offer – Facebook, MySpace, Twitter, StumbleUpon etc.

Widgetop

widgetop.com

Another contender in the battle for your homepage real estate is Widgetop, and there are no prizes for guessing that its primary concern is apeing the Mac OS X Dashboard environment, complete with a Widget bar from where you drag and drop your favourite Widgets as and when you want to use them. As with Apple's Dashboard, hovering your mouse over the little "i" icon on a Widget reveals its preferences, while accessing even more Widgets is done via the **Widget Gallery** link. This web-based tool is also accessible from mobile devices via widgetop.com/mobile.html.

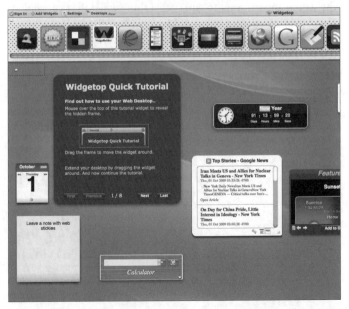

EyeOS

eyeos.com

There are many cloud services out in the ether right now that offer a complete operating system within your browser, and EyeOS is among the best. Once loaded, you have access to a complete cloud-based file system, office applications, a calendar, email client, FTP client, games, and lots more. It really feels like a brand new computer that's just come straight out of the box. The advantage of all this is that your entire computing environment is available to you anywhere that you can find a web browser and an internet connection. Right now, the question for such services is why would anyone want to run such a thing when they currently need a perfectly good version of Mac OS X or Windows to run the browser that runs the OS? Still, it's an amazing piece of kit and well worth a play with.

iCloud

icloud.com

Like EyeOS, discussed opposite, iCloud is the complete package, bundled up into your browser. Anyone familiar with the Windows operating system will feel right at home in this "webtop" environment – complete with Vista/Windows 7-styled Widgets.

Considering that iCloud is free to use, the suite of tools and apps included is very impressive and will almost certainly fit in well with the way you already work. The built-in text editor, for example, is more than happy to deal with Microsoft Word documents. It seems in general to be very Microsoft-friendly: the developers state that iCloud is best suited to being used within Internet Explorer. Put to the test, the overall experience in both Firefox and Safari was slow and twitchy. But if you are happy to work in IE, take a look.

G.ho.st

g.ho.st

Ignoring the gimmicky personalized-numberplate-style web address, G.ho.st offers a feature-rich set of tools, including access to Zoho applications (see p.140) and YouTube. Overall, the feel of this desktop suite might be a little too "XP" for some people, though with an integrated

email application and a generous 15GB of online storage space, this service is worth taking a look at.

Viewing your home desktop

The alternative to using a truly web-based desktop service is to make your own computer's desktop available online. There are several services available that will help you do this, including MobileMe's Back to My Mac feature, LogMeIn and GoToMyPC. Each of these is covered in more detail on p.122, but they do the same basic task of opening a path between the machine you are working on out and about and the machine you have left behind at home or in the office.

Don't expect the world from such services, as they are very much dependent on the performance of the internet connections at both ends (and if you are sat in a coffee shop somewhere using Wi-Fi, that might be too hot). They can also be a pain to set up, as you often have to negotiate network firewalls and mess around with router port configurations. Still, they can be useful and are sure to become far more commonplace and usable over the next few years.

12

Office suites & tools

Workplace web apps

We all require the services of "office" applications at one time or another. Until recently, Microsoft pretty much had the market sewn up with their conveniently titled desktop Office suite (Word, Excel, PowerPoint, etc). But times are changing, and many of the most exciting tools for creating text documents, spreadsheets and presentations now reside in the cloud. Even better, many are free to use.

Google Docs

docs.google.com

Google's free web-based office suite needs little introduction. Even if you don't yet use it, you will almost certainly know several people who do, and if you are a Gmail user you will more than likely have noticed the **Documents** link lurking at the top of your inbox screen.

For those, however, that need a refresher, or are coming to Google Docs for the first time, it's a suite of browser-based tools for creating text documents, spreadsheets, forms and presentations, bundled up with a cloud-based environment where all your documents reside.

You can use Google Docs to collaborate on documents and projects with friends and co-workers to such a seamless extent that multiple people can be working on the same document, at the same time, from different locations around the globe. Though all your files live on Google's servers, they can also be downloaded or emailed in various formats. They can even be shared in an online "read-only" format with anyone who has an email address – you simply send them a link, which is much tidier than messing around with attachments.

Security

Google Docs has become a high-profile target for criticisms about cloud security, and although few large companies feel comfortable yet with the idea of saving potentially sensitive material online, the security that is in place is more than adequate for most people's documents. As with Gmail, Google Docs uses the secure "https" protocol (see p.60) whilst transmitting your data back and forth from the server; if you need more peace of mind, read the help files found at: tinyurl.com/y9twzkj.

Mobile access

There are several mobile versions of Google Docs available as web apps that automatically redirect you to a custom interface when the regular Google Docs address is entered into a mobile browser. Though you don't get anyway near the functionality of the experience you get from a regular browser, you can view documents and also edit spreadsheets.

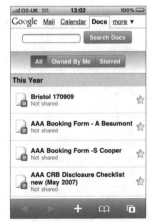

Zoho

zoho.com

Zoho are keen to stress that data security is a big part of what they are about. They state that their data centres have "…on-premise security guards, security cameras, biometric limited access systems, and no signage to indicate where the buildings are, bullet proof glass, earthquake ratings, etc". The company is right to be as public as it can about its security credentials, especially as they are clearly looking to attract big business to the cloud with their corporate service. Of course, this is all good news for us individual users too.

Though not as widely known as Google Docs, the Zoho web-based office suite boasts an impressive armoury of weapons. As an "individual" user you have access to a free version of every tool, while there are also premium applications ready and waiting for the business community. As with other suites you can share documents and edit collaboratively in real time. Here's a quick overview – in alphabetical order – of the tools that you are likely to find the most useful (though also take a look at the site for a complete rundown):

▶ **Zoho Notebook** An amazingly rich note-taking tool that can handle audio, video and images as well as text.

▶ **Zoho Planner** A handy calendar tool with integrated to-do lists and, again, useful tools for collaborative work online.

▶ **Zoho Projects** A very useful project management tool that integrates with Planner. The free version only allows one project at a time, while the paid-for version has various extra features.

▶ **Zoho Sheet** A spreadsheet application that runs as both a web app and a desktop Widget.

▶ **Zoho Show** A presentation web app that can import PowerPoint documents, and can also be used to present your finished work remotely.

▶ **Zoho Wiki** An amazing tool for creating and maintaining collaborative wiki websites.

▶ **Zoho Writer** A word processing package (pictured below) with support for Microsoft Word documents, among other formats.

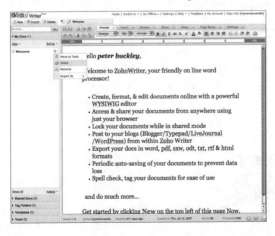

Office Live Workspace

workspace.officelive.com

At the time of writing, the Microsoft Office suite is only available as a suite of applications that has to be installed on your computer. They do, however, have a cloud version in the pipeline, and the web-based Office 2012 tools are expected to see the light of day sometime soon (hopefully before 2012).

For now, then, Office users will have to get their online fix from Office Live Workspace, a web-based environment for storing and sharing Office documents between multiple users. There are some useful tools for setting preferences for sharing for individual files and the system lets you see when others are editing, or have edited, particular documents.

EditGrid

editgrid.com

Flexible, fast and feature-rich, EditGrid is a seriously good browser-based spreadsheet creation tool. If you've ever used Excel, you'll feel right at home, and will more than likely find that you prefer the EditGrid interface to that of Microsoft's ubiquitous Office application.

The tool is free to use on an individual basis, while businesses can sign up for a free thirty-day trial before being asked to pay for the service.

As with many of the other sites covered in this chapter, the key attraction is the possibility of collaboration. Individual files can be shared with other users in several ways, and also published directly to websites and blogs.

SlideRocket

sliderocket.com

This dedicated presentations package is a very impressive piece of kit. As well as allowing you to upload your own content from your desktop machine when building presentations, it also integrates horizontally with other internet resources – so, for example, you can import pictures directly from your Flickr account (see p.182).

Where SlideRocket scores the most points, however, is its interface, which is an absolute pleasure to use: everything works intuitively and quickly, and the folders and tagging tools make it very easy to keep track of projects and their associated resources. And because you can run your presentations directly from the web, you don't need to take anything with you when you go to meetings – all you'll need is access to a browser.

Web-based writing

If you are looking to get some writing done, we have already seen
that you can easily do so using Google Docs (p.138) or Zoho Writer
(p.140). However, there are also several dedicated writing tools to be
found in the cloud. Here are a few worth checking out:

▶ **Buzzword** buzzword.acrobat.com
Buzzword (pictured below) is a very slick offering from Adobe (the company
behind Photoshop and Acrobat). It's easy to get started with – you simply sign up
for a free Adobe account, which can be used with their other web-based software too (see p.151) – and there are plenty of options for customizing your text.

▶ **WriteRoom** writeroom.ws
This is designed to be a distraction-free writing environment for those whose
concentration easily wanders; there's also an iPhone app version.

▶ **DarkCopy** darkcopy.com
Another tool for writing without the distraction of email, eBay and the like.

▶ **Luminotes** luminotes.com
A simple, free and effective tool for creating a personal wiki notebook.

Dimdim

dimdim.com

Though you wouldn't guess from the name (unless I am really missing something), Dimdim is a web-based conferencing tool. It could in theory end up saving you quite a bit of cash if you regularly host long-distance phone-based meetings. Once you have an account set up, simply click **Host Meeting** from the Dimdim website, play with the available options and then invite people to join you. Other people attending your conference can either join the meeting using the Dimdim website or, alternatively, dial in using the provided number. The voice audio side of things is handled by VoIP (see p.87), the same technology that Skype uses, but you also get to enrich your conferences with video, desktop sharing and an interactive whiteboard.

For free you can host conferences with up to twenty people; for anything larger you will need to sign up for one of the "pro" options.

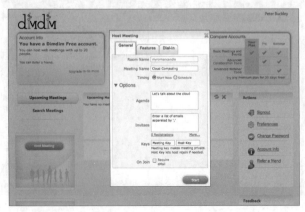

Twiddla

twiddla.com

Another browser-based whiteboard meeting tool is Twiddla, which is both free to use and requires no account setup procedure to get started (though with a paid-for subscription account you do get more control over

the privacy and security settings of your meetings and you can also save the finished results).

You can try the service out by joining the public "sandbox" meeting that's permanently running. Alternatively, to invite people to a meeting in the unregistered "guest" mode, you simply send out a web link. The whiteboard tools are easy to use and fun, and the audio quality that you can expect to get from your meeting is excellent.

If you happen to be having a meeting that's discussing a website, one very clever function enables you to pull that website into view and then start scribbling and jotting all over it – simply enter the site's URL in the address box on the Twiddla toolbar.

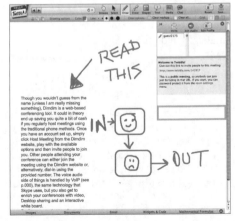

Creately

creately.com

Charts and diagrams are what Creately is all about. The interface feels a little retro, but it all adds to the charm of the site, and the impressive array of options and palettes is anything but old-fashioned. The learning curve is steep, but once you discover the wealth of templates to get you started, you'll be knocking out flow charts and circuit diagrams like a pro. As with so many web-based applications, collaboration is a selling point, and inviting people to either view or help with diagrams and charts is painless. Once you've finished, you can export your masterpiece as an image, PDF or as XML.

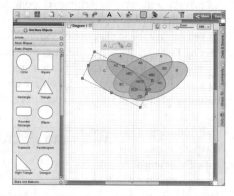

Font building

This has nothing to do with web-based baptisms but instead is all about creating your very own personalized typeface using a nifty cloud application called YourFonts. You download and print out a sheet with spaces for all the individual characters you need to build a font, use a good old-fashioned pen to fill in the boxes, and then scan and upload the results to the site, which then generates you an instant OpenType font.

YourFonts yourfonts.com

13

Messing with images

Editing photos online

Professional photo-editing software has traditionally been the preserve of the professionals. But in recent times, even free software given away with digital cameras has let you fix red eye or remove an unwanted uncle from wedding snaps. Many incredibly powerful photo-editing tools are now finding their way online, and most can be used for free, right from your browser. This chapter shows which are the ones to play around with.

Pixlr

pixlr.com

In contrast to Adobe's offering (see opposite), Pixlr's browser-based image editor is undoubtedly designed to ape the ubiquitous Adobe Photoshop desktop application. All the palettes, menus, effects, layers and option bars work in a very similar way, with the end result being an impressive piece of kit. You don't even need to create an account or hand over any cash to use it (though you should hit that **Donate** button if you like the app, as they have most definitely earned it). To get started, simply open the webpage, upload a file, and get stuck in. This really is an invaluable tool for designers and professionals who need the power of Photoshop but might only have a web browser to hand.

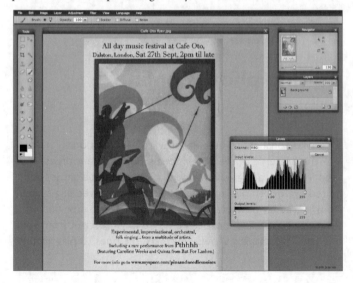

Photoshop.com

photoshop.com

Photoshop.com is accessed using a free Adobe account
(mentioned elsewhere in this book in relation to Buzzword; see
p.145). You get 2GB of cloud storage for your images and a set of
tools for editing and making minor adjustments to the material
you upload (or pull across from Facebook, Flickr, Photobucket or
Picasa accounts).

Anyone familiar with Adobe's fully featured Photoshop
desktop application (part of the expensive, design-industry-
standard Creative Suite) might feel a little short-changed by what
Photoshop.com has to offer. What Adobe have cleverly done,
however, is stripped the interface back to the basics, to give a very
useful set of tools and options for getting the best from regular,
everyday photography, but without overcomplicating things.

Converticon

converticon.com

This is neither the most exciting piece of cloud technology in existence nor the most impressive to behold, but it is incredibly useful. Anyone who has ever needed to create icons for use on their computer (for customizing a file or folder, say) will tell you that resizing and exporting them to the correct dimensions and format can be a fiddly business. Converticon does the hard work for you, and all from the comfort of a web browser. Upload an image file, set your dimensions, and save your icon. It's a real time-saver.

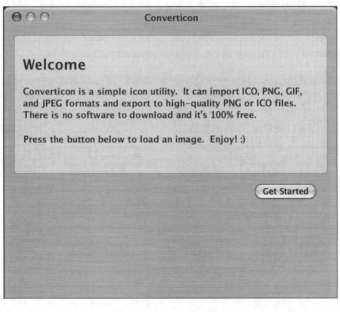

Crop & Resize

caricaturesoft.com/online-tools/crop

With cloud computing tools, you can squeeze all the bells and whistles in the world into a browser frame, but if the actual experience is lousy then none of it will be worth bothering with. If the tool in question fulfils a real need and gets the job done quickly and efficiently, then that will be the site or service that you come back to again and again. Crop & Resize is a case in point. It's free to use, very fast, and does exactly what it says on the tin (and a couple of things that aren't on the tin too – you can add text to images and also rotate them).

The same company also offers a free tool for creating stylized "cartoon" versions of uploaded images.

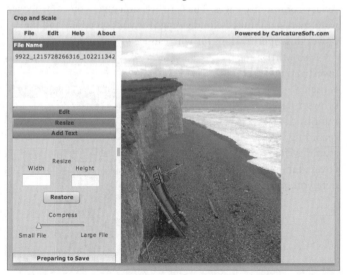

Phoenix

aviary.com/tools/phoenix

Aviary is a name to watch out for in the world of cloud computing; the company's online suite of tools is excellent and features some pretty sophisticated graphics tools, including Raven (a vector editing app similar to Adobe's Illustrator), Toucan (a colour editing package), Peacock (a graphic effects tool) and Phoenix (their fully fledged image editing tool). As with Pixlr, the palettes and toolbars in Phoenix are similar to those in Photoshop, though with even more attention to some quite advanced tools – such as masks and layer effects. The basic version is free to use, though your finished files will have an Aviary watermark on the bottom corner and will all end up on public display within Aviary community pages. The "pro" version gives you control over watermarks, unlimited cloud storage for your creations and the power to set permissions for who can view your images.

Also worth investigating is their browser-based multitrack recording studio, Myna, covered in more detail on p.174.

Picnik

picnik.com

Like the aforementioned Photoshop.com (see p.151), Picnik is
an image-editing package aimed at the casual user. The available
tools are displayed along a single toolbar along the top, and each
process is explained in detail to help you get the best out of your
images. For a couple of dollars a month you can also go "pro", to
use more advanced tools and effects. Picnik also recognizes that
we do all now keep a lot of images online and need somewhere to
tweak the levels and make minor colour adjustments. Integration
with other photo library sites is swift and painless, allowing you to
get your paws on images stored with Facebook, Picasa, MySpace,
Flickr, Photobucket and more. You can alternatively upload files
from your computer, or even connect to an attached webcam and
take a snap there and then.

FotoFlexer

fotoflexer.com

If you can overlook the fact that the buttons and icons on this site feel a little bit chunky and pre-school, the tools on offer are actually excellent. Effects, distortions and decoration filters all work well and the "fullscreen" mode makes it really easy to work without the distractions of your browser or the site's banner ads.

Even better, there is no registration process to slow you down (though you will need to sign up to access some functions); you can simply upload a file, make the changes that you want to make and then resave it back to your computer. But that isn't the only export option. You can also publish images direct to sites such as Photobucket, Facebook, Flickr and SmugMug; alternatively, you can send the file in an email or save it to the FotoFlexer servers and use a direct URL address to retrieve it.

14

Notes & scrapbooks

Capturing the moment, capturing a thought

Computerized note-taking has come a long way in the last few years. The Internet has helped a new generation of cloud-based tools to develop that are much more than just a few virtual Post-it notes on your screen. On the simplest level, the joy of cloud-based notes is that they are always available to you, anywhere that you can get online. And at their most advanced, they can help hold onto your ideas and organize your life, through audio, photos, text, web clippings and much more besides. This chapter takes a look at the most interesting propositions out there.

Evernote

evernote.com

Evernote is arguably the best note-taking tool available on the web right now, given that it can create notes from text, images, audio and even whole webpages. All these notes are then synced between the Evernote server and whatever desktop or mobile versions of Evernote you are running. So, it's your choice whether to run Evernote as an application on your computer – there are versions available for both Mac (pictured opposite) and PC – or keep everything in the cloud and use the web app version on their website via a browser.

By far the coolest feature of Evernote is the fact that images you add as notes are uploaded, processed, and then become searchable by any text in the images; the upshot of this is that it becomes a brilliant way to quickly and efficiently gather information using a phone's camera – snapping the covers of books you want to remember in a store, say, or the names of artists displayed on a gallery wall.

When it is this easy to harvest notes and information, being able to filter and search your archive is important, and Evernote provides a ton of useful features for that too.

Evernote comes in two flavours: there's the free version, which allows you a monthly upload limit of 40MB; and a premium version which gives you 500MB. Though the upgrade is only $5 per month (or $45 per year), you're best off playing about with the free version first to get a feel for how quickly you use up

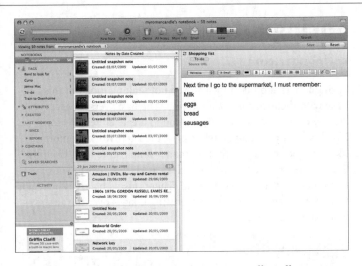

your quota. As you might expect, photo notes will swallow your bandwidth pretty fast, while sticking with text notes will stretch your usage allowance further. However you want to play it, there's a handy usage monitor, so you always know how you are doing.

Evernote, out and about

There are various Evernote mobile apps available to download and install. If you use either an iPod touch or iPhone, head to the iTunes App Store and download the free app: it has an unfussy interface, and is particularly useful for posting photo-notes over the airwaves. BlackBerry Curve, Bold and Storm also have a fully featured app available in the BlackBerry App World: its voice memo feature is very slick and it lets you add files to notes as attachments. The Evernote Palm Pre app is also worth looking at, and can be downloaded from the Palm App Catalog. For more on all the available mobile apps and also download links for Windows Mobile versions, visit: evernote.com/about/download/#a-mobile.

Springnote

springnote.com

Springnote is another fully featured note-taking tool, but this time with the focus on collaboration. The basic version gives you 2GB of online storage and the option to create either "Personal Notebooks" or "Group Notebooks" – the latter working more like a project-management tool than a simple note tool. Usefully, Springnote projects can be backed up as HTML files to your computer for extra peace of mind. There's also a handy iPhone app for reading pages on the go and posting images over the airwaves when out and about.

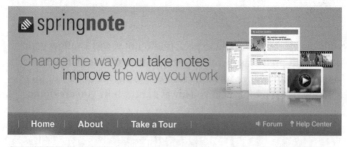

OpenID

OpenID is an interesting alternative to traditional forms of password management. Websites that sign up to OpenID can turn to a third party (an Identity Provider) to confirm your credentials when you want to log in to their sites. What benefit does that actually have for the average user? Well, it means that you don't have to remember hundreds of pass-words, and also means that data related to your online identity is stored with fewer sites. For a video introduction to the process, see *tinyurl.com/yeovzeq*, or vist the OpenID website at *openid.net*.

übernote

ubernote.com

This free-to-use note-
taking service offers
unlimited storage
capacity and has a
very user-friendly

web-based interface. It furnishes you with tags to organize your
notes and provides an "auto save" feature, which means you can
simply get on with your brain-dump and let übernote worry about
the rest.

You can also add attachments to your notes and make them
available for sharing with friends, or make them public for the
world to see. More useful still, there is a plethora of ways that you
can post and view your notes:

► **UberMail** Submit notes via email to a personalized email address.

► **UberMark** A very useful bookmarklet for remembering favourite
websites.

► **UberClip** The übernote web clipping bookmarklet can save
sections of webpages as notes.

► **Firefox Toolbar** Lets you add (and view) notes, but also create
clips from webpages.

► **iPhone and Mobile** Use übernote from your mobile.

► **iGoogle Gadget** Add, view and edit notes from your iGoogle
homepage.

Scrapblog

scrapblog.com

If your passion is the traditional art of keeping a scrapbook, then you might well enjoy putting aside the glue and scissors for a while to take your hobby online. Much more than just a standard blogging tool, Scrapblog incorporates a decent armoury of web-based image-editing tools (opacities and reflections are on offer as well as the usual crop, rotate and zoom controls). The main drag-and-drop interface is called the Scrapblog Builder, and this is where you put your pages together. It's a hefty Flash-based piece of kit, and can be quite slow to load, but once up and running the experience is really good.

The service can work in parallel with image-hosting sites such as Flickr (pictured below), MySpace, Picasa, SmugMug, Webshots and Photobucket – so if you already use one of these, it is by far the easiest way to get your images into Scrapblog. You can, of course, also upload resources straight from your computer, which then appear in the left-hand resources panel alongside imported snaps from other sites.

Moving things around on the page is a lot of fun, and there are loads of themes, backgrounds and

To retrieve your images from a site such as Flickr (pictured), you will first need to authorize Scrapblog to access your account with the other website.

frames available to liven things up – though be careful not to get too carried away, as things can get pretty cheesy pretty quickly.

Once you have created your finished pages, you can either save them online as part of a private collection, publish them for fellow Scrapbloggers and friends to see, or if you want something tangible, you can even order high-quality prints of your creations. You can also export JPGs and download high-quality versions to print out yourself.

With multiple pages created, you also get to view and publish your scrapbook as a slideshow, complete with animated effects, music and transitions between pages.

More scrapbooking tools

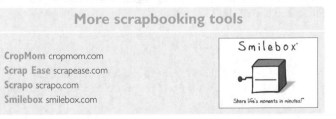

CropMom cropmom.com
Scrap Ease scrapease.com
Scrapo scrapo.com
Smilebox smilebox.com

Posterous

posterous.com

Similar to Twitter (see p.190) in principle, Posterous is a micro-blogging site but like many of the best cloud resources, it blurs the lines between different functions. This tool could easily have been filed under "blogging" or "social networking", but instead it is being dealt with here, with all the other note and scrapbooking tools, simply because it performs that function very well too. Once you have your feed set up, you can start adding text, photos, audio clips, web clippings and documents, and use the mobile version to take photos from your phone and post them to your page. If blogging is your primary concern, you can also use Posterous to autopost everything you add to your other accounts; it integrates with numerous services, from Twitter and WordPress to Blogger, Flickr and TypePad.

Netnotes for Firefox

This nice little Firefox add-on can be used to add notes on specific websites to your Firefox bookmarks. Find it at: *addons.mozilla.org/en-US/firefox/addon/8658*.

Part 4: Play in the cloud

15

Cloud music & video

Online services that change the way you watch and listen

While the battle between the music industry giants and the illegal file sharers rages on, it's good to know that there is a raft of innovative services out there looking to rethink the way that music and video are delivered, whilst also keeping us punters on the right side of the law. In this chapter we'll take a listen to some of the best and see what they offer.

Last.fm

last.fm

Last.fm is a great way to discover and listen to (and watch) new music for free – so great, in fact, that more than thirty million people have signed up. When you set up an account, Last.fm starts to keep track of what you listen to in iTunes and on your iPod – including your listening history. This information is analysed – "scrobbled" – and Last.fm starts to serve up custom streams of tracks based on your taste. The end result is somewhere in between your own personal radio station and the iTunes Genius feature.

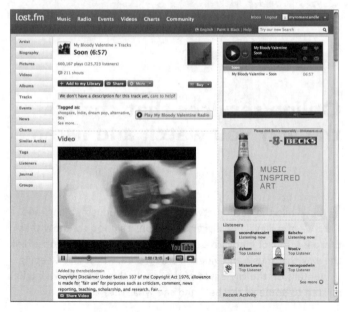

The legal situation

The various ground-breaking cloud music services covered in these pages are collectively competing with both commercial online download stores (such as iTunes) and – arguably more significantly – with illegal downloading made possible by P2P (peer-to-peer) file sharing.

Some years ago, legal action saw one of the most prolific file-sharing sites, Napster – the first major P2P system – disappear before eventually resurfacing as one of the larger legitimate online music providers. The music, film and software companies continued to fight back. In 2005, the Recording Industry Association of America (RIAA) and the Motion Picture Industry (MPI) were successful in closing down the company behind the Grokster P2P program. Many other file-sharing sites have also toppled; but newer sites and technologies appear in their place, the most significant at present being the Bit Torrent networks that enable even faster downloads of massive files, which have quickly become the latest nemesis of the movie companies.

In the meantime, the music industry, led by RIAA, has focused on individual users. Quite a few file sharers have now been prosecuted, but with millions of people using file sharing, the record companies simply can't go after every one of them.

Spotify, meanwhile, manages to stay on the right side of the law by passing on payments to the record companies in respect to the music streamed and monies made. Whether this will fully satisfy the music industry remains to be seen, as some record labels have allegedly already threatened to remove their songs from the service, claiming that they have not received that which is owed to them.

The interesting twist in the story is that sites such as Spotify and Last.fm point to a future where our music resides in the cloud and we pay a subscription to use the internet as an always-on, completely customizable radio service. But would people be prepared to give up their MP3 service? History says "yes" – a few years back we were asking the same question, but in relation to CD and vinyl collections. And if, say, Apple introduced a subscription service to the iTunes Store, that could be the start of something big. Only time will tell.

Spotify

spotify.com

Spotify lets you stream content from an online archive in a similar way to Last.fm, but this time via a downloadable application (available for both Macs and PCs). In exchange for the privilege, you have to put up with the occasional audio ad, or – for a monthly fee – go ad-free. Though it is undoubtedly a conceptual leap to go from having your own offline music collection to exclusively using an online resource, you do benefit from an always-on stream of music that you like. There are also mobile versions of the software available for iPhones and Android handsets.

Flavortunes

flavortunes.com

This cloud-based tool sets out to democratize your disco by sending special invitations out to friends prior to a party, complete with a proposed playlist, and then asks them to vote for the selections that they would like to hear. Come the night of the gathering, the cuts with the most votes then end up on your Flavortunes playlist and the music is streamed to you over the Internet. Friends can also make requests for specific songs to expand the scope of your initial list.

Simplify Media

simplifymedia.com

One of a raft of applications and services that strive to untether your music collection from your desktop machine, Simplify Media basically allows you to stream music from one computer over the internet to other computers with the software installed (either Mac or PC). And assuming that iTunes is your jukebox application of choice, the new shared library simply pops up in the iTunes sidebar – it's easy to set up and works like a charm.

The service also allows you to stream your personal photo collection across the internet and you can even invite up to thirty friends and family members to share all your media – assuming of course that they too have the software installed. In short, you are setting your library up as a streamable internet radio station for a select group to enjoy.

There are also a couple of mobile apps available from the iTunes store for viewing photos and streaming music to iPhones and the iPod touch. The sound quality isn't perfect over 3G or EDGE networks, but it's top-notch over Wi-Fi.

BlueTunes

bluetunes.net

Like Simplify Media (see opposite page), BlueTunes is all about making your music collection available to you whenever and wherever you are. But where Simplify Media streams your media from your home computer, BlueTunes actually takes your whole collection online. Though this can be a cumbersome process to set up (as all your songs have to be uploaded), the end result is that your collection is safely stored in the cloud rather than on your desktop machine – protecting it from harm should your computer ever die on you or get stolen. This might well have the knock-on result of freeing up a considerable amount of room on your home machine – which is really what cloud computing is all about.

The service is free to set up, though you do need to register and create an account. The BlueTunes web-based jukebox software is very usable, and the service also allows you to stream your music to iTunes and share it with friends and family via Facebook. There is also an iPhone web app (pictured below) that allows you to stream music to your phone over the airwaves.

BlueTunes certainly has an interesting approach, but one wonders whether this start-up ultimately has the muscle to survive in a market dominated by the Apples of this world. Worth playing with nonetheless.

blueTunes meets the iPhone

Now, even the biggest music library fits on any size **iPhone** or **iPod Touch**.

1 Sign up **here** and select what songs to upload.

2 Go to **blueTunes.net** from your iPhone (there's no app to purchase/download).

3 Carry your **full** music library in your pocket wherever you go.

Myna

aviary.com/tools/myna

Checking emails and creating business presentations on the move is one thing – but can music production actually be done via a web browser? Myna is an amazingly powerful multitracking audio studio for recording, arranging, mixing and exporting. Even those already acquainted with cloud tools will be impressed with this one.

There are some decent enough effects (delay, reverb, flanger, etc), along with controls for volume, balance and gain. Importing samples is easy and you can download your finished masterpieces or share them with other members of the Aviary community.

Best of all, it feels really solid, and even responds to keyboard shortcuts, which is essential when quickly scrubbing back and forth in your mix.

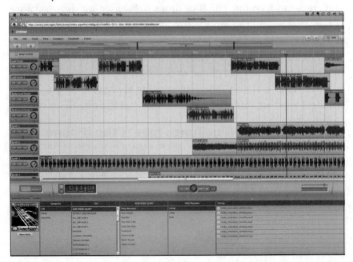

Hobnox – Audio Tool

hobnox.com/index.1056.en.html

The Audio Tool from Hobnox is among the most fun and impressive cloud creations to be featured in this book, and will appeal to anyone who may have messed around with guitar pedals or vintage drum machines in their youth. The webpage gives you a beautifully rendered array of pedals, tone generators and beat machines that you can then patch together to create complex chains of effects – twiddling the knobs and clicking the pedals on and off changes the sound you hear in real time – making this an instrument that could actually be used in a live setting.

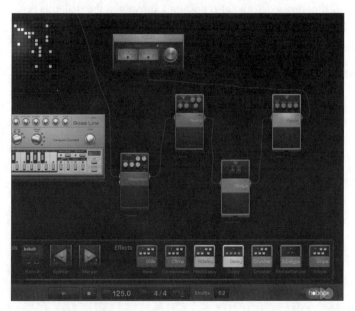

YouTube

youtube.com

YouTube is no doubt familiar to most readers as the place to go to find video clips online. But there is more to it than that. Once you have logged in (YouTube is owned by Google, so you can use your Google account credentials to get started), YouTube can also be a powerful online tool for both aggregating and sharing your favourite clips and also uploading and storing your own movies to create your very own "channel", which can either be kept private or opened up for the masses to view.

Given that so many mobile devices these days are capable of shooting video and also posting it directly to the web, this is becoming a popular pastime. While many channels dish up mind-numbingly tedious cellphone footage of young teens trying to do tricks on skateboards, there is also some great stuff on YouTube worth searching for. And if you want to start raising the quality a tad, start posting your own masterpieces.

Silentube

Silentube is a clever little browser bookmarklet that lets you watch YouTube videos without all the surrounding baggage of the YouTube site; while it's certainly not something that's ever going to transform your universe into a shining palace of gold, it does have its uses. Find out more via *silentube.com*.

iPlayer

bbc.co.uk/iplayer

It has taken a while, but finally the world is starting to realize that TV and the internet make great bedfellows. The net allows TV programmes to be unshackled from the schedules and made available to us when we want them. The BBC's iPlayer (UK-only at the time of writing, though it can be viewed with Boxee in the US; see p.179) is among the best web-based players online right now, and there's also a downloadable piece of software that can be used to save particular programmes for offline viewing.

There is also an excellent mobile web app version of the site available at bbc.co.uk/mobile/iplayer, which works brilliantly over Wi-Fi, but does not work over cellular data networks.

Hulu

hulu.com

Hulu is a web-based TV streaming service that pulls together content from a ragtag fleet of US TV networks, with NBC Universal in the flagship position. The browser interface is really nice and the breadth of available content is good. At the time of writing, Hulu is only available to view by residents of the US, though a UK version of the service is in the pipeline and should be available some time in 2010.

A couple of years back, Hulu content was also freely available to stream through the Boxee software (see opposite), though in recent times the relationship between the two services has been somewhat rocky. Similar to the Boxee offering, Hulu are also developing their own standalone application to take the user out of the browser and into a dedicated media centre environment.

Boxee

boxee.tv

Boxee is a free-to-use media centre application that lives on your computer (it's available for Windows, Linux and Mac machines) but seamlessly integrates with the cloud to dish up internet TV streams from many of the major US networks, feeds from YouTube, MySpaceTV and MTV, Apple movie trailers, iPlayer content (see p.177), and a whole lot more. You can also use the software to browse your Flickr or Picasa photo libraries and aggregate RSS streams.

When you get started with Boxee you have to set up a user account – a necessary step, as the service has a strong community aspect to it, with users being able to rate content and make recommendations to friends over the network. You can even export your watching habits as a continuous feed to sites such as Twitter, Facebook and FriendFeed.

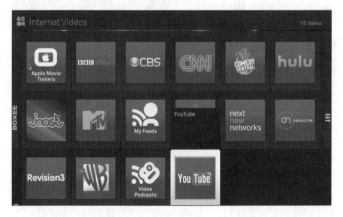

Shazam

shazam.com

Finally, this is one of those
services that to some might
seem like a simple gimmick,
but to others is incredibly
useful. Once you have the
mobile app installed (of which
there are versions available
for Android, iPhone and
BlackBerry), you can use
Shazam to identify almost any
piece of music that you hear
playing in a club, bar, on the
radio, anywhere. It works by
taking a sample of the music
via your phone's microphone
and comparing the audio's
"acoustic fingerprint" to
those stored online in a cloud

database of songs. It then dishes up the song details for you to
wow your friends with.

16

Photo clouds

Keeping your photos online

I f your computer was stolen tomorrow, what would you feel most upset about having lost? Your music? Or perhaps all your family photos? If it's the latter, then it's time to seriously think about moving your precious snaps to the cloud. There are numerous services available, some with basic free packages and others that require a subscription if you want anything like a reasonable amount of online storage. Then there's functionality to think about. Do you want to make online slideshows, or use preferences for sharing and commenting perhaps? This chapter looks at a number of the most popular sites online.

Flickr

flickr.com

Flickr has become the most popular and well-respected online photo community. Owned by Yahoo! (you can use a Yahoo! ID to log in), the site hosts billions of images for both professionals looking to show off their wares and amateurs who just need somewhere to store and share their snaps.

The basic free account puts a cap on the number of images you can upload each month, and also only allows you to view the most recent additions to your "photostream", so anyone remotely serious about the service will more than likely switch to the "pro" version pretty quickly. This gives you unlimited storage space and uploads.

Flickr also has an excellent slideshow function (pictured below), and a special web app for tagging and naming images and then organizing them into "sets".

MobileMe Gallery

apple.com/mobileme/features/gallery.html

Bundled in with the MobileMe subscription account, the
MobileMe Gallery is accessed via me.com (click the sunflower
icon at the top of the page) and offers a rich user experience,
though without the community functionality found in many of
the other sites and services in this chapter.

Images can be uploaded to the Gallery direct from an iPhone
and preferences can also be set so that friends and family can
either add their own pics to your collection, or download your
shots for themselves via a browser. Slideshows are easy to set up
and the whole thing synchronizes in both directions very well
with iPhoto in OS X. The MobileMe Gallery, like iPhoto, is not
limited to use with images, and can also be used to store and view
movie files, either synced from iPhoto or uploaded from a video-
capable iPhone.

Picasa Web Albums

picasa.com

Google has a free standalone photo application called Picasa; it's available for both Mac and PC and is an excellent program, just as good as either of the bundled offerings that Microsoft and Apple ship with Windows and OS X respectively.

On the cloud side of things is Picasa Web Albums, which can either be used to sync specific albums from Picasa, or employed as an independent online tool for managing uploaded photos. Google give you 1GB of space to play with, there is a very good slideshow tool built in and you also get a Google Maps preview of where a selected image was taken (assuming the metadata is embedded within the images you upload, which it should be with either a GPS capable phone or camera). For anyone who already uses Gmail or other Google services, Picasa's web incarnation is a good choice as it's easily reached via the **Photos** link at the top of Gmail, Google Docs and Google Calendar pages.

SmugMug

smugmug.com

SmugMug is a professional-looking, cloud-based photo community site with a gorgeous interface (complete with themes to customize your look), really polished slideshow and gallery tools, full-resolution photo storage and previewing (many sites downscale your images when you upload them to save space) and unlimited storage capacity.

There's a free trial version, but if you want to continue using the site you will have to part with some cash. At the time of writing the first rung of the subscription ladder is $39.95 per year, which for anyone who is serious about their photography is arguably a price worth paying.

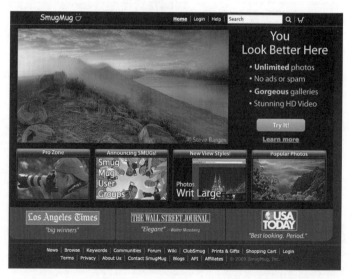

Photobucket

photobucket.com

Free to use, Photobucket is for many the repository of choice for hosting images displayed on social network sites such as MySpace and Facebook as well as shopping sites like eBay – hosting your eBay product images "off site" means you don't have to pay extra fees for adding multiple pics to a listing. This is a useful resource and can be a handy way to ring-fence images you want to cross-post to other community sites away from your main online photo collection.

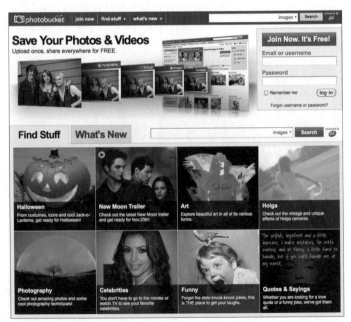

17

Social networks

Making the most of online communities

Though sites like MySpace and Facebook seem to have been on the scene forever, it is only recently that they have started to find their feet as genuinely useful cloud tools. The initial excitement over the arrival of a platform that allowed you to look at pictures of people you might once have gone to school with has subsided, while the rise of Twitter has caused all the key players to take a look at their specific offerings. This chapter briefly looks at a handful of the more important services and what their contribution to the cloud amounts to.

Facebook

facebook.com

Love it or hate it, it seems that Facebook is here to stay. Compared to similar social networking sites, it has so far shown itself to be resilient enough to withstand the shifts in online fashion and adaptable enough to employ new fads and gimmicks (Twitter, for instance) to its own ends. It has achieved all this by becoming the primary means by which many people communicate and present themselves online. Is it a cloud computing service? Yes, absolutely

– and more than any other site in this book, it's the one place where you really do conduct a degree of your actual social life within the cloud.

Here are just a few of the ways that Facebook has become a first port of call online for so many people:

► Communication
Facebook's messaging system is easy to use and great for invitations and event organizing; it's far better than email for many purposes. Couple this with the messaging "Wall" and "Pokes" and you have a pretty powerful set of tools.

► Micro blogging Facebook featured a "What's on your mind?" box and status updates long before Twitter was on the scene, and this feature remains incredibly popular with many users.

► Photo posting Facebook offers unlimited image uploads (which is more than the free versions of most photo storage sites give) and allows you to tag both yourself and friends in images on the site.

► Boxes A little like the iGoogle homepage, the "Boxes" page features drag-and-drop-style Gadgets and apps that create additional functionality.

► Mobile access Aside from browser access, there are mobile versions of Facebook available for the BlackBerry, iPhone (pictured), iPod touch, some Nokia phones and also Android handsets.

Twitter

twitter.com

Twitter falls somewhere between a social networking service and a mobile blogging tool. It allows you to broadcast SMS-style posts of up to 140 characters (and as a result is often referred to as a "micro-blogging" service). These individual "tweets" – like the status updates found on Facebook – are typically used to describe what you're doing or thinking at any one time. Other users can become your followers, which means they'll be able to read and reply to your tweets, and you can in turn follow them, or anyone else you happen to come across on the site.

Despite historic problems with its servers, Twitter has shown itself to be a medium perfectly suited to mobile use, with smartphones such as the BlackBerry and iPhone having had numerous third-party apps developed for the purpose. For example, the iPhone app Tweetie (pictured) allows photo posting from the phone's camera and location-specific twittering from GPS-enabled devices. There are also plenty of standalone Twitter clients available for both Macs and PCs which take Twitter out of the browser and into a continuously updated feed window. The ones worth trying are:

Snitter getsnitter.com (Mac & PC)
Tweetie atebits.com/tweetie-mac (Mac)
Twhirl twhirl.org (Mac & PC)

Having started as recently as 2006, Twitter looks set to multiply its population very rapidly over the coming years, with both individuals and organizations keen to use the RSS-like nature of the service to make themselves heard. It remains to be seen, however, if Twitter can survive without either a subscription charge or any onboard advertising.

Follow me...

Here are a few Rough Guides twitter feeds to get you started:

twitter.com/PeterBuckley
twitter.com/RoughGuides
twitter.com/RoughGuidesTech

LinkedIn

linkedin.com

With a population of well over thirty million registered users and a demographic that falls into the 25- to 45-year-old age bracket, LinkedIn is a business-oriented network that is becoming increasingly popular. It operates by allowing its members to maintain a network of "trusted" contacts, or "connections" within any given industry, and as such can be an excellent networking tool (in the traditional, real-world sense of the phrase).

To be added as someone's connection, you need to receive an invitation from another member; the value of this system is that you can make contact with individuals you may not know directly, but can trust by association. There are also several mobile apps available for LinkedIn and various useful community tools, such as LinkedIn Groups (topic-based discussion and networking groups) and LinkedIn Answers (a great way to get answers, normally of a professional nature, utilizing the expertise of the wider community).

FriendFeed

friendfeed.com

Now that you have created a cloud life for yourself, it's time to turn to FriendFeed (owned by Facebook) to pull all the disparate parts of the content you consume together. The site is a well-designed aggregator for RSS feeds, micro-blogging streams, status updates and the like, and it can be customized so that you only get exactly what you want and don't have to go trawling around loads of different sites to read the posts and blogs you are interested in.

There are plenty of ways to connect with FriendFeed beyond the browser: your feed can be added to Facebook as an app or to an iGoogle homepage (see p.129) as a Gadget; there are numerous mobile apps; and you can also receive your feed via email, Twitter or IM.

If you don't get on with FriendFeed, you can get a similar end result with Plaxo (see p.76).

Second Life

Created by Linden Lab, Second Life (*secondlife.com*) is not so much a social networking site as an entire virtual world, complete with clubs, shops and real estate. The idea is a variation on the Massively Multiplayer Online Role-Playing Game (MMORPG) genre made popular by titles such as EverQuest and Ultima Online. Instead of hunting for treasure and battling demons, however, Second Life offers a world more similar to our own in which users – called "residents" – can interact.

Second Life isn't a simple website, but a full program that you need to download and install, though the fabric of the virtual world is stored online in the cloud. Each user has an avatar modelled after themselves or some fantasy version thereof, and can do anything from visiting a nightclub to starting a business. Most more involved things – such as buying land and building a house – require payment with Linden Dollars, which have a real-world value.

Second Life does run on Macs and Linux, but some features only work well on Windows.

Maps & more

These are a few of our favourite things...

To round things off, here are a handful of sites and services that really capture the essence of what cloud computing is all about, but don't quite fit into any of the other chapters of this book. Maps get a special mention as they fit brilliantly with the new generation of web services and mobile devices that are coming through – they let you pinpoint your exact location and ask the question "what's nearby?"

Google Maps

maps.google.com

It's pretty hard these days to do anything online without Google Maps popping up somewhere; but few people take the time to fully explore the Google Maps pages and unlock the wealth of information that they contain. Once logged in with your Google account details, take a look at the left-hand sidebar, where you can add a default location (perhaps where you live); also investigate the **Get Directions** and **My Maps** links to create custom maps that you can come back to again and again.

From the upper-right corner, click **More** to reveal icon links for Wikipedia entries, as well as posted photos and videos. And click **Traffic** for live traffic updates – a feature also found on several mobile versions of Google Maps.

Finally, there is the controversial "Street View" (pictured below left), which had the world's media up in arms with concerns over the public's privacy (glass house? … stones?). The feature gives you a navigable, road-level view of various cities around the world and is accessed by dragging the little orange man from his perch atop the main navigation slider (if he appears greyed out, then no Street View is available in that area).

Google Earth

earth.google.com

Though Google Maps can be viewed in "Satellite" mode through a browser, the best way to experience the full possibilities of Google's mapping endeavours is with the standalone application Google Earth, which is available for download for PCs, Macs and the iPhone. The application itself does not contain all the data, so you still need to be online to use it.

The Google Earth community is very active, with enormous amounts of new data being added daily. One easy way to get involved is to use the application's "touring" feature (click the camera icon on the toolbar to start), which lets you record virtual journeys around Google Earth, which you can then furnish with a soundtrack and share with friends or the community as a whole.

But the scope of Google Earth is not limited to either terra firma or the twenty-first century – you can also go for a stroll on the Moon or Mars, under the ocean, and even in Ancient Rome.

Loopt

loopt.com

Loopt is an online community-based service that for many might just be a step too far in terms of personal privacy. This mobile app (available for, among others, iPhones, Android handsets and BlackBerrys) lets you see which of your friends are nearby (assuming their phone is switched on), giving their exact location on a map. From there you can use it as a tool to meet up and find places to eat or drink nearby (via content dished up by Yelp – see opposite). There is also a web version of the service so that you can see who's where from a browser.

At the time of writing Loopt is a US-only service that works with most of the major network carriers. If you're outside the US, you might like to try Google Latitude (google.com/latitude), a similar service that's available in the UK and elsewhere.

Yelp

yelp.com & yelp.co.uk

Trading beneath a banner that reads "Real People. Real Reviews", Yelp is an online community that looks to review real-world establishments – mostly bars and restaurants, but also shops, banks, pharmacies and even petrol stations.

As a signed-up member of the community you get to post your own reviews, which will be available to read on the website along with those of other users. But where Yelp gets really clever is with its iPhone app, which presents results on a map that shows your current location and what's around you. Once you have pinpointed the place you want to go, you can bookmark it, email a friend and send them the location details, take a photo to post, or draft a review to add to what's already been posted.

The Yelp iPhone app also features a secret experimental "augmented reality" function (you have to shake your phone three times for it to appear) that allows you to view the world via your iPhone's camera and see the Yelp listings overlaid on the screen (pictured below).

Glue

getglue.com

Glue is a community-fuelled recommendations engine for books, films, video games, restaurants, music, etc, that integrates with Firefox as an add-on and gives you suggestions of things that you might like to read, watch or listen to. The suggestions it presents you with are based on the preferences and choices of others within the community and also on the items you have already tagged using the Glue bar that pops up at the bottom of Firefox when you are browsing the web. The Glue bar cleverly understands what kind of site you are viewing at any one time and makes suggestions in the appropriate media. In many ways it works similarly to StumbleUpon (see p.108) and, indeed, features a **Shuffle!** button that furnishes you with a random selection – the more you tag, the more tailored your recommendations become.

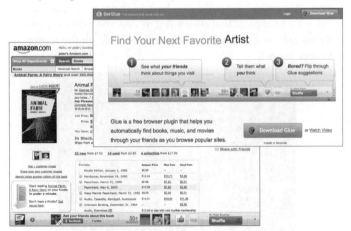

JamLegend

jamlegend.com

Internet gaming has been around for a long time, and there are literally thousands of online games that could have been picked on to fill this slot. JamLegend gets a mention, however, both for being an amazingly addictive implementation of the *Guitar Hero*/*Tap Tap Revenge* school of tap-along gameplay, but also for its community aspect. You can challenge anyone to a duel and slowly work your way up the rankings until you get to see your name up there under the heading "The Jam Legends". You can also throw your own compositions into the pot – which is a great way for bands to promote their tunes.

Scribd

scribd.com

Scribd is an online community for sharing documents – think of it as a cloud-based publishing portal awash with original creative writing, recipes, maps and much more. You can get started by uploading any number of file formats (Word, Excel, PDF and PowerPoint are all supported) and adding them to your profile. The majority of the material within the community is there to be read online, though some publications can also be bought and downloaded via the Scribd Store.

Index

Index

index

index